THE PETERS THIRD BLACK AND BLUE GUIDE TO CURRENT LITERARY JOURNALS

Complete with Whips, Kisses, Scalpels and
The Noisome Bunny Awards

With drawings

by

MEREDITH PETERS

Dustbooks Editions
1987

Drawings throughout by Meredith Peters

First edition.

ACKNOWLEDGEMENTS

To Charles and Pamela Plymell, of Cherry Valley Editions, who launched the first *Guides*. And to Len Fulton, editor of *The Small Press Review* where several of these essays appeared earlier in much abbreviated versions, in my column "The Peters Black and Blue Guide."

Dustbooks
Box 100
Paradise, California 95969

TABLE OF CONTENTS

JOURNALS EXAMINED IN EARLIER GUIDES

GUIDE I

ABRAXAS
APR
ANTAEUS
BOXCAR
CHELSEA
CHICAGO REVIEW
FIELD
GEORGIA REVIEW
HUDSON REVIEW
IOWA REVIEW
KAYAK
KENYON REVIEW
THE NEW YORKER
OHIO REVIEW
POETRY
POETRY NORTHWEST
POETRY NOW
PUSHCART PRIZE: VII
QUARTERLY REVIEW OF LIT
SALMAGUNDI
SHANANDOAH
SOUTHERN POETRY REVIEW
SOUTHERN REVIEW
TELEPHONE
VIRGINIA QUARTERLY
WORMWOOD REVIEW

GUIDE II

THE BELLINGHAM REVIEW
BLUEFISH
BOGG
CONNECTICUT POETRY REV
CONTACT II
ELECTRUM
GRAHAM HOUSE REVIEW
GRAND STREET
GYPSY
IRONWOOD
MAGAZINE
MASSACHUSETTS REV
NEW LETTERS
THE PARIS REVIEW
PERMAFROST
THE POETRY REVIEW
PULPSMITH
SAMISDAT
SULFUR
TELESCOPE
THREE PENNY REVIEW
YELLOW SILK

Copies of the first two GUIDES are still in print, and available from Cherry Valley Editions, Box 303, Cherry Valley, NY 13320. The first guide costs $4, the second $5, plus $1 for postage and packing. Orders are promptly filled.

BOOKS BY ROBERT PETERS

Poetry

FOURTEEN POEMS
SONGS FOR A SON
THE SOW'S HEAD AND OTHER POEMS
EIGHTEEN POEMS
BYRON EXHUMED
RED MIDNIGHT MOON
CONNECTIONS: In the English Lake District
HOLY COW: Parable Poems
COOL ZEBRAS OF LIGHT
BRONCHIAL TANGLE, HEART SYSTEM
THE GIFT TO BE SIMPLE: A Garland for Ann Lee
Founder of the Shakers
THE POET AS ICE-SKATER
GAUGUIN'S CHAIR: Selected Poems
HAWTHORNE
THE DROWNED MAN TO THE FISH
CELEBRITIES: In Memory of Margaret Dumont
THE PICNIC IN THE SNOW: Ludwig II of Bavaria
LUDWIG: The Acting Version
WHAT DILLINGER MEANT TO ME
HAWKER
KANE
SHAKER LIGHT
LUDWIG OF BAVARIA: POEMS AND A PLAY
THE BLOOD COUNTESS: POEMS AND A PLAY

Criticism

THE CROWNS OF APOLLO: Swinburne's Principles of Literature and Art
PIONEERS OF MODERN POETRY (with George Hitchcock)

THE GREAT AMERICAN POETRY BAKE-OFF: First, Second, and Third Series
THE PETERS BLACK AND BLUE GUIDES TO CURRENT LITERARY PERIODICALS: First, Second Series, and Third Series

Editions

THE POETS NOW SERIES OF LIVING AMERICAN POETS: Scarecrow Press
THE LETTERS OF JOHN ADDINGTON SYMONDS (with Herbert Schueller)
LETTERS TO A TUTOR: THE TENNYSON FAMILY LETTERS TO HENRY GRAHAM DAKYNS

In Memory of KENNETH REXROTH

"By and large, writers are not very nice people . . . There are too many piglets, and too little swili in the trough . . . ."

--Kenneth Rexroth

FROM THEIR MOUTHS YE SHALL KNOW THEM

"...so I forgot the main thing / like when you spot a fly in the room...."*Jack Myers*, CRAZYHORSE.

"...my butt is beginning to ache."--*Lewis Turco*, THE FESSENDEN REVIEW.

"She saw her head out."--*Sue Gangel*, HOW(Ever).

"these bounce off / and around / like dumb ideas"--*Hart Schultz*, THE FESSENDEN REVIEW.

"I learned not to fear the body I came from."--*Cheryl Clarke*, HANGING LOOSE.

"We must each lose an arm . / I know you would agree, and / smile."--*Anne Schwendiman*, FRANK.

"i roll over to write this."--*Tim Robbins*, HANGING LOOSE.

"Sometimes I feel sometimes...."--*Derek Walcott*, HARPER'S

"A sense of the self starts in the mouth and spreads slowly."--*Rae Armantrout*, HOW(Ever).

"Ho, but it is dirty."--*Elizabeth Bishop*, HARPER'S.

"Tie large dead animal to rear fender"--*James McGlyn*, THE NEW YORK QUARTERLY.

"If I trace silence / some will say I trace nothing."--*Theodore Enslin*, ORIGIN.

I know I'm small & nothing will happen...."--George Evans, ORIGIN

"Me and my friends like summer and baseball games."--*Debra Kay Vest*, PIKESTAFF.

"It's not a dead little thing / without a spinal chord yet...."--*Molly Peacock*, POETRY.

"What need do we have / with two ears, / two nostrils, /two penises?"--*Gerald Locklin*, POETRY L/A.

"my cock crowed and crowed and crowed."--*Al Poulin, Jr.*, OUTLAW.

"Not even a dog shits in his own house."--*Jim Heynen*, OUTLAW.

CRITICS COMMENT ON THE FIRST TWO *BLACK AND BLUE GUIDES*

"Peters is in top form--hilarious, insightful, outraged, outrageous, and unique....He is the best, most thorough commentator we have on the entire poetry scene."--*Brown Miller,* THE SAN FRANCISCO REVIEW OF BOOKS.

"...a scintillating survey of the current scene with lots of quotations and names, giving one a real sense of what is going on, good and bad."--*Judson Jerome*, THE WRITERS DIGEST.

"...an immensely useful tour by a knowledgeable insider of the current 'po-biz' scene filled as it is with names, dates, and facts useful for the cultural historian."--CHOICE.

"The general reader who enjoys feisty, pizzazz-type criticism will love these books. After the smoke dies down, what is left is often accurate and incisive stuff."--*Doris Grumbach*, SMALL PRESS.

"Peters is a harsh critic. Read this volume and come away roaring."--*Robert Hauptman,* LIBRARY JOURNAL.

"Better to be released by Peters pounding a stake through your heart than haunt ivy-covered graveyards as one of the Undead."--*Steve Abbott,*CONTACT II.

"Peters' tastes are eclectic. He responds positively to well-written poetry wherever it appears...."--*J. Ferlazzo*, CHOICE.

"He's supportive of the raw, the rough, the honest, the experimental and minorities. In the hothouse of contempo American poetry he's made himself the critic they love to hate. Good for a sunny afternoon of snickers, snarls, and a sartori or two."--*CITY PAPER* (Washington DC).

INTRODUCTION

In this new GUIDE, my third, I examine twenty-one periodicals, returning only to look again at *Poetry* , first examined in the first GUIDE. Nearly all of the journals are national in scope. My earlier design remains: to scrutinize a selection of journals both fledgling and hoary, both rambunctious and conservative. Again, in the interests of space, and to reflect my own interests, I eschew fiction, and most essays and reviews. This decision remains difficult, for we certainly need acute assessments of lit mag prose. My own poems have appeared in over a hundred journals to date, and my essays would increase that number greatly. It seems unfair to penalize those editors who have liked my work enough to publish it. I realize, of course, that my subsconscious self tips towards those journals; yet, I hope that by being clear about this I am a responsible critic. Some magazines publishing me receive Noisome Bunny awards and a fair birching; others publishing my work are kissed and blessed. I have appeared in HANGING LOOSE, HOME PLANET NEWS, MID-AMERICAN REVIEW, THE NEW YORK QUARTERLY, POETRY AUSTRALIA, POETRY /LA, and THE REAPER.

My audience remains three-fold: 1). Librarians who seek guidance through a maze of literary magazines. My three GUIDES, to date, assess over 70 different journals, and provide librarians with assistance in determining which of this wealth of material are worth subscriptions. 2). Poets looking for outlets for their work. By reading the GUIDEs they may save themselves much postage and effort by determining which journals are apt to give them a careful reading: alas, many of the better-known organs publish poets already published, or their coteries, or poets from the Writing Programs and a handful of trade and university presses. 3). The host of poets who have appeared in the earlier guides. Over a thousand such writers have received my comments, some extensively, some less so. Those who are scrutinized negatively are apt to be poets with, I think, inflated reputations, coterie figures who pass the prizes, grants, and workshop appointments around among themselves. A negative take will scarcely do more than ruffle a few feathers, as the subjects proceed on their merry ways to sinecures, prizes, and fame. I am aware also--and this has happened (I can supply text, chapter, and verse)--that by making adverse judgments of these quarterlies, and of individual poets they publish, I am closing off outlets for my own work. So be it; I shall remain grateful to those editors and poets who see the importance of my writing, particularly of the poetry itself. My criticism always remains handmaiden to my poetry. In fact, my hope is that readers stimulated by the reviews and essays will read the poetry.

One trend that bothers me much is ageism: the darling poets of these journals are almost exclusively under fifty years of age--the ripe decade runs from, say, 35 to 45. Another problem is that the most exclusive of the journals feed at the hog-troughs of public monies: POETRY, THE AMERICAN POETRY REVIEW, CHIAROSCURO, and CRAZYHORSE among them. I suggest that all such monies be withdrawn until and unless these editors prove that they are responsive to a broad spectrum of poets, including minorities.

My taste is eclectic. I am just as excited by poems in old forms (old Swinburne and Tennyson lover that I am) as by new and experimental ones. This may not, of course, appear to the casual reader to be the case--I can only ask for his indulgence, and encourage him to read between the lines. I continue to do battle with most that the ANTAEUS-POETRY-APR-AWP-NEA-WESLEYAN-PSA-ATHENEUM AXIS represents: the Ego Poem trivialities from a poet's life; the Old Folks at Home poem--excursions into sentimental memories of family and friends; a poet's cute rites of passage to manhood or womanhood; the Coy Bucolic vapid imitators of William Stafford and Robert Frost; the "You" poem, which fills in some imagined or resurrected YOU with news they should already know; the Dying Relatives poem; the Reportage Style, in which poems generate themselves around tedious journal entries--the Day Book Poem is one of the disasters to appear in the past decade or so; and there is as always, The Academic Abroad Poem. My efforts to whack the bottoms of poets who write these poems badly will seem obvious. I hope, finally, to upset, amuse, and titlllate--sufficiently to send readers off in quest of the journals and the poets to discuss, to see if and where I have erred. Certainly, I hope to encourage and provide models for young poets not yet ossified into Workshop or Summer Writers' Conference Clones. My wish is that even those disagreeing with me will appreciate that I have tried to substantiate my judgments by evidence from poems themselves. My models as always go back a ways, to Thomas Carlyle, A. C. Swinburne, D. H. Lawrence and, more recently, to Kenneth Rexroth and to Robert Bly.

Once again, Meredith Peters' drawings embellish the book. If we were really up-to-date, the cover design of harpies typing at their Selectric with their toes (harpies don't have hands) should feature a Word Processor. The AWARDS colophon of the shaggy child holding a dead rabbit by its ears is a humorous effort to propel poetry to the realms of the Oscars, the Emmmys, and the Tonys. May Noisome Bunny Awards prevail! The better the magazine, the fewer noisome bunnies it receives.

■

Robert Peters
Huntington Beach, California
April 1986

■

Meredith Peters
The United Nations Library
Geneva, Switzerland

CHIAROSCURO

Nos. 3 and 4: 1983,1984. Editors: John Latta and Chris Henkel. 108 N. Plain St.,Ithaca, NY 14850. Yearly. $9 for 2 years.

When these copies of *Chiaroscuro* arrived unannounced in my mail, I looked forward to a treat, for a number of poets I admire appear here: PATRICIA GOEDICKE, ROBERT MORGAN, JAMES HEJNA, and ANSELM PARLATORE, among others. What I find is a pretty dull feast, with a special emphasis on the bland, both in theme and mode.

The direct experience, first-person poems seem always interchangeable poet with poet. Give yourself a happy mix of Relatives Poems--for dads and kids particularly, so ubiquitous in journals spawned by APR/Iowa. Give yourself sentimental feelings. One poet as he sits "at the center of an immense desire," hears hydrangeas breathe. Another observes a "little tugboat" leaving a harbor "bound for dreamy obsolescence." Yet another drifts with sadness and hopes "to sit under a tree with its dusty fruit / of salvation." WILLIAM MATTHEWS flattens a cute take on himself, "skinny" and "serious" standing beside a "frankly" squinting pig as "foursquare as a bathtub." In another dull piece "A Long, Hard Year," Matthews spins a feeble joke: he sells the movie rights to one hard year of his life for a flick called "*Forever Ember.*" Like most poets here, Matthews is nicely-tooled--there are no tacky enjambments, grosseries, or false feet forward: on first reading, you may feel you are even reading something good. Be advised.

MAXINE CHERNOFF's "A Concise History of the United States" is, at least, "concise." What she produces, though, is kitsch surrealism: her jails "burst with pride," her "blindfolded cowboys" smell "of card games," she eats "pickled breast of sky." None of this goes anywhere. We are left feeling "good," the way old

Tennessee Ernie Ford's songs made us feel: her poem is a "necklace / we wear only gradually."

Elsewhere, JACK DRISCOLL shuffles tamely towards a pod of whales beached "on the first snow in moonlight" near Boston. Only one leviathan remains alive, is moved through the Mystic River, where "a man injects the whale against her secrets," whatever that means. She's on her way to the Seaport Aquarium. Driscoll shifts the view to "spawning salmon" slamming themselves against a wier's steel bars where they are captured and milked of milt" by hatchery men in rubber boots." The old hairy device of the pathetic fallacy allows us to imagine these fish as they "dream a stretch of gravel/they will fan into beds with their flat tails." How do salmon relate to our stranded, captured whale? Both are robbed of their birthright dreams--one via injection, the other by oviparity assisted by gloved fingers. Fingerlings are produced, so the salmon species continues. The whale, though, finds no "breeding ground." Driscoll's parallels fail to *deliver*. Cleverness goes awry, and the reason is that the poet doesn't really care enough. There's a total absence of passion. Nothing remotely suggests that this poem required writing.

STEPHEN KNAUTH writes zippily of life-meanings and gentled nature, viz., those river stones "we try to inflict with intelligence," or those pines, "local buildings of the first order," growing there, so tall, in a spot "where real giants urinate upward/so high the stars hiss (sic)/ & go out... "What all this adds up to is a reminder that "we are loose on Earth / & looking for a place to stand" and, like those "real giants," piss upwards, ie., reach the stars with our human stream. Up there (where is IRVING BERLIN when we need him?) comets are born from "red-haired women." We are meant to believe in all this because the fact of the sun setting inside a wren's throat is as certain "as real/ soup" boiling "magnificently on the stove." On first reading, the congenial comparison reassures me (I'm grateful that it isn't chicken soup); soon, though, the soup turns tepid, a failed image of the sort fledgling poets in workshops write.

A related malady is the chockablock literary phrase which passeth for profundity. BARRY CASSELMAN's "After Volcanoes" is rife with them: "this warm edgeless cloud," "separations between us," "scenes of opaque departure," "simple order in the world," "a prolonged and elegant sleeping," "assays of phenomena," etc. The poem winds off with self-conscious, ill-felt, alliterative gems that take their dull cue from "edgeless," a couple of lines above): "Not angels. No angels.//Illegible intervals."

A father-son baseball poem by MICHAEL WATERS opens with a platitudinous observation that our "selective" memory chooses among "swarming moments." The kid *pocking* the old Spaulding with pa, looks up to see mom in the window, the tutelary (or mammary) spirit of that ostensibly "peaceable kingdom." In part 2, Waters unflinchingly evokes his mother's pain:

her fingers picked
till bright breads of blood
punctuate the white, legible scars,
her raving phonecalls to the police.

That is powerful. But when he again conjectures on memory, he's solipsistic. Nor does a reference to the Talmud help, nor does the one bright spark in the closing stanzas, that leap from the pasture of childhood to the contemporary world of "the roaring, traffic-jammed world." Sentimentality takes over.

There are a some fine poems in these two issues. Three are by JAMES HEJNA, an outsider with no obvious connections to either Cornell or Ithaca House. "I Would Like To Seduce You But I Am In Traction" is the best. Here, Hejna in hospital, unable to move, must content himself with visions and phrases of a "skywriting" he projects over and around the ceiling of his room. The nurse tapes a picture of his lover to his bed. A man nearby dies. Hejna's love and hunger are starkly and potently evoked in these final lines:

Anna McNaughton, your spoken name,
in my voice, as I looked at your face,
filled the small holes that pain
bored in the ceiling. Come visit.
I recover to see you,
wishing: STOPS SUNBURN PAIN.

ANSELM PARLATORE's contributions, two poems from his as yet unpublished "Mecox" manuscript, are unique. No other poet so imaginatively incorporates the language of medicine and with such intense human feeling. Mecox is a huge marshy area near Parlatore's home at Southampton, Long Island, one of the country's major wild-life breeding grounds. "Mecox Affair" opens with an image of boats moving along tributaries:

Gaff-rigged stern-steerers, wind boats, under
sail on Mecox
tributaries frozen, they arrive in separate
cars
past the pond of mute swans

The poet is attending a symposium, and, wearying of "cascading metabolic pathways & membrane pumps," lets his thoughts wander to a couple in some sand dunes. The woman alleviates her sadness via her greenhouse flowers--browallia, begonias, coleus. The husband, feeling the estrangement, adapts an image of fecund, mating lobsters to soothe himself. Estranged birds from the midwest, trapped over winter in the Mecox, hear the same oceanic bird call he does: "*it's alright. Everything will be alright.*" The concluding image of a flounder dropping eggs brings little comfort. An implacable marine life persists:

& how slowly the flounder rearranges its
viscera
twists its skull, one eye moving over to join

the other,
the eggs sinking in clusters to the muddy
bottom here.

Also memorable is CAROL FROST's "All I Cannot," a delicate love poem with an amazing momentum which moves from a clear vision of a lover to an "ebony / fling of darkness." This passage occurs early:

I've seen you
bathing, washing, drying yourself,
your breasts cretonne and right in the basin;
felt your presence in a room long before
you arrived; stalked you with a sort of cold
fever
only by standing silent where a little light
was.

A cursory look at the contributors' notes reveals that *Chiaroscuro* is an unabashed house organ, featuring writers published by Ithaca House. *Chiaroscuro* is an "affiliate." According to my count, of the 58 poets represented in these two issues, 30 have either had books published by Ithaca House, or are folk who have lived (or are living) in Ithaca, with connections at Cornell University, home base for Ithaca Enterprises. Most of the other poets have been published by some of our most conservative, traditional presses: Princeton, Massachusetts, Louisana State, Georgia, and Wesleyan. Many have been kissed by prizes given by such safe groups as AWP, the New York Poetry Center, National Book Critics, and the Guggenheim Foundation. A mere half dozen poets escape these "blessings." The editors do say they invite submissions--but be advised: it does help to have been published by them, or to have a pedigree they will admire. Editors Latta and Henkel describe their editorial policies, in *The International Directory of Little Magazines & Small Presses* , this way: They ride "protectively, Indian style, between a horse of Irrepressible Scoffing and one of Final Amazement and Awe. We would rather be falteringly eclectic than eclectic to a fault." They extol "language finicky and condign and rampant." Here's another instance of editorial flash and dance outdistancing the performance. Hype? Further, they urge contributors to read a copy of *Chiaroscuro* before submitting. As my scrutiny of current contributors reveals, your chances of appearing here are minimal unless you have prior connections with Ithaca House or Cornell. I do not complain of this (many journals showcase their ponies), but hope merely to describe the exact nature of things, in case you may be thinking of sending work here.

CRAZYHORSE

No. 26 (Spring 1984). Managing Editor: Russell Murphy. Poetry Editor: David Wojahn. Dept. of English, Univ. of Arkansas, Little Rock AR 72204. Twice yearly. $8 per year.

The editors of this very slick-appearing journal of poetry and prose invoke a blessing from *Bury My Heart at Wounded Knee*: The world men live in, Crazy Horse knew, was a mere "shadow of the real world." To enter that "real world" one had to dream. There all floated and danced. Crazy Horse's horse then "danced as if it were wild or crazy, and this was why he called himself Crazy Horse." Be warned, if you expect to find anything wild or crazy in these utterly conservative pages, forget it. Once again we hold yet another academic, high-prestige journal, lavish with poets published by the big and the academic presses: Viking, Wesleyan, Grove, Doubleday, Ecco, Houghton Mifflin, Yale, Utah, Illinois, and Louisana State. These poets all have academic connections, are products of MFA programs, and appear in the appropriate journals: *The Iowa Review, Kenyon Review, The American Poetry Review, Virginia Quarterly Review, The Southern Review, Georgia Review, Ironwood, The New Yorker, Poetry, The Nation*--all staid, dull perpetrators of the safe and, occasionally, the inane.

What strikes one after reading the first half-dozen poets is their passivity and fascination with trivial events in trivial lives. To be specific: MAURA STANTON is narcissistic: " . . . see me standing outside the florist's"; the trivial event trivially observed: "A businessman in a camel overcoat / Passes a red-haired girl with a yellow scarf, / And neither will ever see each other again" (the spavined grammar here is Stanton's doing); the enervation: "How accidental my existence seemed." In a second poem, Stanton waits in an airport, having missed her plane--which she watches take off without her. This triviality occasions an embarrasing recollection of her grandmother visiting the World's Fair of 1904. When Stanton tells us that the old soul "never forgot the force of all that light," how does she know? She's jamming thoughts down into the dear departed's cranium, and I am not convinced. The poem concludes on these utterly passive (almost placid) notes: If she'd made the plane

In thirty-three minutes I'd resume my life
With hugs and talk. Instead I look up.
Beyond the lights, the sky is immense.
A few planes dare to cross at intervals
Further and further apart, like canoes at
sea.

LAWRENCE RAAB is trite in set up and also utterly passive. In "Romanticism," he gives us a rainy night (god, how these poets love rain and night!), and a man in a small hotel or boarding house room. As he listens to the rain "he's reminded / of some romantic vista...." I won't bore you with what it is he sees; you can pretty much guess. How do we relate to this dude's loneliness? Raab tell us to calm down, so that we won't "make him feel / too bad, or burden him / with our sorrows."

CHRISTOPHER BUCKLEY also drifts along, draws in an elusive literary word "circumstances," and listens to a seminary bell which "reminds us / how we accept the silences drifting down to us." We too, "in the circumstances / of our ribs and skin" are "thin clay bells / begging a little something from the wind." LOUIS OMAR SALINAS after returning to town, not caring for the "face" of his "anger," winds off vapidly:

And I stand in a corner
a little happier, looking
through the trees,
walking softly in town.

By now we're inured to the casual and the trivial, and JACK MYERS does not let us down. He rambles on with a meditation on "good health," whatever that is. He quits his bad habits, so he can "grow old," contemplates "the nothing" marching both before and behind him, and engages in these boring considerations:

Every bit of consciousness focused on
what was different
so I forgot the main thing
like when you spot a fly in the room
the whole room softens and disappears.

He loves the ugly "like" phrase, the casual bad grammar passing since the 60's as hip--but which, now, alas, is merely tacky. In a second poem there's this: "like when you're on a train...."

KAREN FISH has mastered the enervated wind-off, wind-down. Here is how "Signs Of Life" ends, with a whimper or two barely enlivened by a few casual images from nature, and some thighs and breasts with minds of their own:

And this is what I think of again and again.
You move, you change,
your face becomes thirty-six different women.
Your breast and thighs remain faithful
and indifferent
restful and indifferent. Beyond this
there are only the few stars that throb,
the cornstalks jackknifed
in the early morning snowfall.

One of the most solipsistic poems of all is "Prime" by PHILIP BOOTH. The first stanza has utterly ugly line-breaks, ending as they do with flatulent adverbs and a dull preposition; and "woken" is sub-par Freshman English:

I've been up since black dark, woken again
to Orion's tipped sword, drifted toward
words, thinking beyond constellations to . . . .

Didn't the editors read this? Even the presence of his "dead father" lying under a ripped quilt can't save Booth. When "Sylvia" (I guess it's a coffee shop) opens and he walks down there "to loosen" himself, we hope it's not his bowels he loosens. Booth says he's "a glad damn fool." By their words ye shall know them!

More passivity from T. R. HUMMER, designed in forgettable four line stanzas, lavished o'er with trite night set-ups, viz., "Sudden in the sudden dark beside you..." Also, a poem that drives "You" far down under. I count 15 *you*s or versions thereof in 22 lines: "And nothing will punish you. You are grown now, / A woman. It is yours to choose, You choose, //And you are here." ANDREW HUDGINS confesses that while he "mostly" gets "the sense," he misses "the nuances." And this question: "What am I to make / of what I scrub off my pillowcase?" had best remain unanswered, even if the pillow belongs to the old poet SIDNEY LANIER.

ELIZABETH SPIRES indulges in a trivial orgy of "night" and "darkness" with much heart-throbbing, weeping, and singing. This action, as reported by ROBIN BEHN, is almost incomprehensible: she watches a "you" scan "the private constellations" whilst the "you" sleeps, and you's body "moves up the lighted street" somehow "connecting lamp // to lamp." More dream-night stuff by JULIA MISHKIN; a cute moment: "What cannot be dreamt of lies down on the edge of sleep / and babbles quietly like a brook, / or a thief." In a second poem, she writes of sleep covering up "the curtains of the eyes," neighbors resting on their stoops on "a slow day," something in the woods so noisome that even the animals avoid it, and a final panegyric to the stars:

Only the stars flew down and across
the expanse and the trillion crystals
of frozen air became touchable, almost
light.

There are a few--very few--good poems here. SUSAN MITCHELL leads off with "A Story," a flexibly-written, energetic, harrowing tale of one Indian murdering another in a bar, "in honor of blood." Though Mitchell writes in the first-person, she is sufficiently inventive to minimalize the solipsism. DAVID ST. JOHN, not usually one of my favorite poets, contributes two fine poems--there's no pretentious writing, no facile line-breaks substituting for a lack of feeling. "Meridan" is my favorite. Here we see daughter of a Count who's a junkie:

As she walked ahead of me in her high
chocolate boots
I could think only of her body still muscled
like a
Snake's & how she lay sprawled last night
Naked on the blue tiles of the bathroom floor
& as I stepped into the doorway
I could see the bathtub speckled with vomit
The syringe still hanging limply from a vein
in her
Thigh . . . .

Finally, two by AI conclude the poetry section. She's the rare poet here who assumes a persona, eschewing thereby the shallow self-obsessions most of these poets love, as flies love sticky fly-paper. "Elegy" is a two part presentation of veterans, one from world war I, the other from WW II. The first dies of old age, the second dies during the hydrogen bombing of Nagasaki. "More" commemorates JAMES WRIGHT's dying:

I want my life back,
the days of too much clarity,
the nights
smelling of rage,
but its gone.
If I could shift my body
that is too weak now,
I'd lie face down on this hospital bed,

this icy water called Ohio River
. . . .
I'd hold on, I'd hold
till the weight, till the awful heaviness
tore from me,
sank to the bottom and stayed.
Then I'd stand up
like Lazarus
and walk home across the water.

Despite these half-dozen poems, *Crazyhorse* is a vast disappointment. Once again, if you are thinking of sending work here it obviously helps if you have credentials with establishment presses and journals, or if you are in one of the better-known MFA programs, or if you have already published in *Crazyhorse*. According to my quick scrutiny of the Contributors Notes, only one poet ROBERTA KOZAK lacks these credentials--so we must assume that the unpublished poet has at best a miniscule chance of being published here. This journal showcases poets under forty years of age who have some visibility in the Establishment Poetry world. Alas. There's nothing here, Crazyhorse, old Indian brave, to dance "wild or crazy" over. The journal is a travesty on your horse's good name.

THE FESSENDEN REVIEW

(Vol X:No. 4, 1985). Editors not named. Box 7272. San Diego CA 92107. Quarterly. $10 for 2 years.

This slickly designed and printed review runs to some 100 double-columned pages and ranges over all manner of books by all manner of publishers, with special attention to smaller presses. Normally, I would pay no attention to the *FR*, except to warn publishers and writers against it. If you think your books will get careful treatment here, forget it!

The editors specialize in one-sentence anonymous dismissals of books, particularly of verse. Most of the longer reviews, written I gather by free-lancers who are paid ten bucks a throw, run normally to a quarter page (often less, if you exclude the large type used for headings). No prices for books are given.

Of particular interest is the "New Books In Brief" section, which here(for Nov-Dec) runs to 22 columns and covers 108 books. The same cantankerous mind seems to have written all these notices. He gives stars and hearts for work and design. Books "not worth the effort" earn zeroes.

BOB A. ELLISON's *The Racehorse From Outer Space* has a "garish and dubious humor." The current Pushcart volume is dimissed: "Is Henderson trying to parlay his way into being *The New Yorker* of the bearded and ink-stained set?" JOSEPH HUTCHINSON's verse is "fey" with "a few unfortunate symbols of the Block-That-Simile school." TED KOOSER "is given to poetic gorpism...." JAMES SCHEVILL's *The Invisible Volcano* garners zeroes ("Not Worth Rating") for design and content, and this "review": "Where do all these poetry books come from? Where are they going? What does it all mean? What's that spot on your shoe?" LYN LIFSHIN's *Kiss The Skin Off* (the reviewer gets the title wrong) is commended for writing titles that are "poetry."

RICHARD PEABODY's *Echt & Ersatz* . . . is "fun in layout...but truly so-so in the poetry department." CHARLES PLYMELL's Selected Poems *Forever Wider* inspires a vicious "forky-dorky" parody:

Names drop in your margins, Plymell,
Like droppings from a sick gooneybird:
Burroughs, Kerouac, Corso
Ferlinghetti, Rod McKuen, and...
ROD MCKUEN? Plymell--what have you done
You beat Beat you?

The reviewer gives STEVE RICHMOND's *Earth Rose* three stars--and then calls GARY SCHROEDER a poetaster who is "just pissing the wind." PAUL MARIANI's *Poetics: Essays on the Art of Poetry* is called "fine and honest," though the reviewer misspells Mariani's name. He likes HART SCHULTZ's *Wesley,* saying that the poems have "nuts" and "something called life." I read the following woeful passage, quoted to show Schultz's qualities, dip in my finger, sniff it, and find that it noisome:

Wesley feels like a
tricycle left
in the yard

it is hailing
the size of baseballs
in Idaho

these bounce off
and around
like dumb ideas...

JOHN YAMRUS, not one of our quality poets, is thus shafted: "It's entirely possible that Yamrus sits down and jaws with the tape recorder, then gets someone to type it up and mail it out as a Poetry Book. We yawn when he writes...." GARGOYLE's fat, seminal *Fiction/84)* is dismissed with 7 words: "A magazine...disguised as a book." My own *Second Black and Blue Guide* is generously if briefly noted, although my daughter Meredith (she supplied drawings) is listed as *author*. My GREAT AMERICAN POETRY BAKE-OFF receives shorter shrift. I doubt that the reviewer bothered to read any of the latter, as I doubt that many of the books reviewed here were more than touched, daubed with skid-marks, and tossed aside. JACK MYERS' and ROGER WEINGARTEN's wretched (I think) anthology NEW AMERICAN POETS OF THE 80'S receives high marks, and praise goes to some of the worst poets there. Japanese poet MUTSUO TAKAHASHI is dismissed for his "wretched excess in gay poetry." And so on. And so on. Some reviews seem to be of books made up for the occasion. A particularly delightful one is *Aunt Erma's Country Kitchen & Bordello*," by FABIAN WORSHAM. As is customary, *FR* merely quotes a few lines--this they do for books they like. I'm not too sure about this one though:

In my spare time I read *The Total Woman* and
spend my afternoons sewing bells on my
underwear.

When my husband arrives he chases me around
the furniture and I jingle like Santa's
sleigh.

An occasional review hits the mark. One is of A. D. WINANS' *The Reagan Psalms*. After "years in a sea of words," Winans "has yet to distinguish the great from the good, and the funny from the boorish." Winans ignores "the oldest rule of all in satire: . . . you must love your hero enough to hate him, must give him wings to fly--so you can shoot him down with a finely-crafted arrow." Touché. It is possible to write a capsule review that says something. And here is a "school" of poetry I wish I had discovered: it appears in a one-line commentary on *Asleep In A Wildflower Sanctuary,* by LYNN EVERETT CORNELISON. She writes "acid-in-the-mountains" and "love-in-the streams" school poetry.

My quarrel with this wretched *Review* is not that it trashes poets I like (including my own work), but that few poets good or bad are treated with care. The best "reviews" simply quote a few lines from a poem and eschew commentary. An occasional review glimmers with substance: ie., one by LORENZO W. MILAM, which is sensitive and worth reading, on a volume of haiku. In an earlier issue there was a lengthy, negative assessment of ROBERT PENN WARREN which provoked outrage in a reader--his letter is published here. What reads like a first-draft prose piece by poet LEWIS TURCO is a sheer waste of space. The opening, badly written, flashes easy exact rhymes: "chair," "bare," "squares," "where," and "chair." We don't much *care* that Turco's ass hurts from sitting. Later on, a book of poems by Turko receives a rave review. I've read it, and it ain't all that good.

What bothers me most here are the faceless reviewers (none of the short takes is signed). So, authors and publishers be warned. Sending review copies here will be a waste of books and postage. If you are a poet seeking outlets for your work, why bother--very few poems are published, and judging from the samples are mostly woeful.

And they do publish a few poems per issue: there's a nasty bit of doggerel by CHARLIE KRAFFT shafted at GARY SNYDER and called "Turtle squirts." "Me and Clyde" go "singing a song / in search of Gary Snyder." They get loaded on grass, drink some whiskey, and "finally" meet "ol' Gary." They are invited in:

We were having a time
Drinking his wine
Even musing about his old lady.
The gang was all there
In their jeans and long hair
When the scene got a little bit shadey. (sic)

Well, Snyder kicks the dudes out (because they are such lousy spellers and doggerel writers?). Their nose-thumbing response?

Outside the door
We could hold it no more
We had to unload that bad karma.
So we yelled back in glee
As we watered a tree,
"Piss on you bums of the dharma!"

So, that takes care of the Gary Snyder haters. AL HEFID's "Jesus Under Water" is another matter--it's a good poem. I don't know thing one about Hefid (he's translated by JEFFREY SHEWMAKER), but I'll keep watching for his work now. He takes one of the hoariest, potentially most sentimental, topics, the nature of Jesus Christ, and writes with originality:

I've been told that Jesus came on a dung-
colored mule
His beard moving in the wind a bloody rose
His feet dripping across the thighs of a mule
They called "Agnes Dei."
They say his eyes were clouded like the wind
That beat across the Kyzyl Kum Desert;
They say that if you listened closely,
You could hear his heart beat and beat and
stop
Like the wind that beat
Across the desert.

Jesus broods on the paradoxes of His life, laments the killing of humans by other humans. Riding "a gold-and-ivory" winged lion, He leaves the earth. His bones are discovered

Turning like the silver spiders at the mouth
Of the river.
The natives in their divine simplicity now

Worship the waters as god. They give over
their ashes,
Their gold and dung-colored liquids to the
sacred river
They refer to as The Sign Of God's Good Grace.
That's where they found
What was left of his black bones
Spinning round like hands reaching
Spinning like hands reaching out.

A third poem, thankfully brief, by MARY DEDERER, "Emily's Pregnant," luxuriates in abstractions and clichés: "this sorrow," "a weight sinks," "thoughts comfort me," "wind blows up her skirt," and "something moves in the dark." The latter might be the Holy Gost coming to impregnate her. We don't know, although the closing image of Mary Magdalene pouring her hair over "His feet" invites us to Bible-up the verses.

Elsewhere, there's a vivid trashing of GUTZON BORGLUM; a piece by DOUGLAS CRUICKSHANK (is he the editor?) on RICHARD AVEDON; a stunning photo by Avedeon of a nude, bald male covered with honey bees; and a frustratingly superficial piece on the painter WILLIAM SIDNEY MOUNT.

FR is one of several small magazines I decided to support this year. I considered requesting my subscription money back, but decided instead that I'd rather pay them for not sending me any more issues.

FRANK: AN INTERNATIONAL JOURNAL OF CONTEMPORARY WRITING AND ART

(I:4 Summer–Autumn 1985). Editor: David Applefield. Advisors: Edouard Roditi and Gregory Masurovky. Either 6, rue Monge, 75005 Paris, FRANCE, or Mixed General Delivery, APO New York 09777. 100 pp. 4 issues for $15.

Frank is a new and lively journal of the arts with a fresh international slant. It's lavish with graphics, and provides a good mix of fiction (very brief dips into novels, including a piece of the editor's novel *Once Removed*), poetry, plays, essays, and reminiscences. Letters are photographed and reproduced (KENNETH REXROTH, PAUL GOODMAN, and ALLEN GINSBERG). A special feature on "Writers Who Draw" presents work by MICHAUX, FERLINGHETTI, KUNDERA and BUKOWSKI, among others. Bukowski's is a delight, and contains a special poem. An excerpt from WILLIAM S. BURROUGHS' forthcoming book of essays *Misogyny and Other Essays*, demonstrates yet again that Burroughs writes boringly self-indulgent prose. Here are some of his profundities: "the written word is an image"; "Journalism is closer to the magical origins of writing than most fiction"; "Any writer who cannot hear that word [Death] is not a writer"; "the word is a virus."

Among the best graphics are a painting by LAWRENCE SPINGARN; a haiku and collage by CHARLES HENRI FORD; a photograph of lesbians making love by MATTIA BONETTI; a frontal nude photo of CHARLES RAY acting as a "Shelf" at a sculpture/performance; and an acrylic by PAMELA WYE of a woman's severed head lying on a beach--her eyes are wide-open, she is calm, and three nude men busily inspect her.

Of special value is "My Female Brother," by MARINA TSVETAIEVA, the Lesbian Russian poet of the 1920's, most of whose work remains unpublished.

EDUOARD RODITI supplies a brief reminiscence of Tsvetaieva and her lover NATALIE CLIFFORD BARNEY. Here is a moment from "My Female Brother":

> **But it is always the desperate desire**
> **only of one of**
> **the two women, of the younger one, who is**
> **most *she*. The**
> **older one needs no child: she has her younger**
> **friend to**
> **satisfy her maternal instincts: "You are my friend,**
> **my God,**
> **my everything."**

Dominating this issue is the commemorative "Homage to Eduoard Roditi at 75." RODITI the avant garde poet, interpreter of OSCAR WILDE, and literary historian remains as energetic and original as ever. Many of the photographs, letters, and documents here are from the UCLA archives. Among the contributors are PAUL BOWLES, KENNETH REXROTH, BENJAMIN PERET, BARBARA HOWES, CHARLES HENRI FORD, LAWRENCE FIXEL, LAWRENCE SPINGARN, and ALLEN GINSBERG. MAURICE GROSSER provides a full-page portrait in oil of the literateur. One hopes that this delicate and sensitive commemoration inspires some energetic bibliographer to produce a full and complete bibliography of this multi-talented man, while he is still with us.

The poetry is the least exciting art represented here. DEREK WALCOTT's poems are faint-pulsed. His "Salsa" makes for unpleasurable reading (even if we overlook this spelling of pomegranate, viz., *pommegranate*): he's dropped in enough names to kill off any sinuous music. "Tomorrow, Tomorrow" is uninspired Surrealism, easy MAGRITTE. ANNE SCHWENDIMAN's prose poem on cutting old friends out of a photo is better: "The cut becomes clear; we must each lose an arm. / I know you would agree, and/ smile." ALBERT MOBILIO writes clumsily, viz., "a child is a murdered face / coupled to the sky's last stars." RANDALL POTTS mixes things fresh with things self-consciously arty. He fantasizes on three women, the first in a photograph (1934) by EDWARD WESTON, another of a Spanish dancer whirling to "guitar & tambourine song," a third speaking to him over the phone:

> **drawn through**
> **twelve blocks of General Telephone cable**
> **your voice sparks**
> **a lipsynched vision**
> **culled from a dozen memories**
> **the bare minium (sic) illusion.**

JAMES LAUGHLIN contributes a throwaway on Cordelia and her "dear old dad." And GARRETT WHITE's "American in Paris" is a tissue of hollow, jaw-breaking phrases: "tremors of density," "The mystery of life," "distances are infinite," "paroxysms of doubt," etc. Like the poet's heart, this poem is "the sentimentalist functioning, *in vacuo*.

Yet, despite my fussings, *Frank* gets high marks for elan, scope, readability, and for featuring neglected writers. *Frank* represents what the stodgy PARIS REVIEW might be but isn't.

HANGING LOOSE

 # 47 (spring 1985). Editors: Robert Hershon, Dick Lourie, Mark Pawlak, Ron Schreiber. 231 Wyckoff St, Brooklyn, NY 11217. Thrice a year. $6.50. $12 for 6 issues.

Hanging Loose is almost 18 years old. Its focus is eastern: the only poets here west of Pennsylvania are WILMA ELIZABETH MC DANIEL from California, TIM ROBBINS (a real discovery) from Indiana, and SY MARGARET BALDWIN from New Mexico. 12 of the 24 poets are from New York. There's a healthy mix of males and females, youngsters and oldsters, and minorities--blacks, latins, gays and lesbians. A standard feature is poetry by high schoolers.

Most poems reflect a casual tone--the "I" poem dominates. One of the most lavish users of this dull device is CHERYL CLARKE. Note her leaden, meaningless line-breaks, which seem to eschew nearly all lyrical quality, maintaining the precise effect of prose chopped into little pieces:

> **I know now I could have told him anything,**
> **instead in the panic of ecstasy**
> **I learned not to fear the body I came from.**
> **I touch myself and faded color prints**
> **project themselves against the screen of**
> **memory....**

Rarely do the poems in *Hanging Loose* tax one's mind or feeling sufficiently to require a second reading. SUZANNE BERNHARDT writes of a "black shaggy dog" that's so dumb, once he climbs out a window, "onto a flat black tarpaper roof / overlooking / the playground" he doesn't know how "to let himself / back / in." The spavining (sprawling) of the lines simply doesn't work.

There's little cerebral, formally innovative, or

otherwise abstruse. The poems pull you in via reportage, viz. these first lines: "He bought a motorcycle," "Letting go is hard"; "It was summer," "I remember our house," etc. And there are several Folks Dying Poems, particularly Old Folks. Here KIP ZEGERS does a triple whammy--uncle, dad, mom. Catch the ingeniously bad grammar of line #2:

My uncle, half blind with cataracts,
old since I have seen him last,
can hardly see what he is propping with a
beam.
My father, his wife in hospital...

Hanging Loose does though publish many poems in distinctive voices. The most harrowing are by EMMETT JARRETT on the death of his wife:

she looked in the mirror last night
saw her steroid-swollen face
and thinning hair
her mouth was a hole full of pain
tears poured out of her endless eyes

KATHLEEN AGUERO's "Helping Grandma To Bed" is a poignant rendering of profound human love. In a lighter vein, JACK ANDERSON's "Retirement" pictures a retired couple who "make every day/ a Sunday drive for a Sunday dinner." PHILLIP MAHONY's Brooklyn street poems ring true--the bio notes say he's a Brooklyn cop. His Fabien is a sixteen year old lock picker, who cracks locks that college grads "with trench coats / and microchips" say are unpickable. Once this street genius is busted, though, illiteracy compounds his problems:

Tonight, as he signs his fingerprint cards,
one sees that same devotion,
that same pride in his work
as he concentrates on each painful letter.

F... A... b... i... E... N...
"What about your last name?"
asks the pot-bellied cop.
"I can't do that one,"
whispers Fabien.

TIM ROBBINS, a sophomore at Indiana University, moves impressively towards personas other than his own. Here is the whole of "two friends":

across his forehead
solitary hairs join heavy eyebrows.

his sleeping breath is heavy and dark.
it approaches and passes.

in the rankled street cars scuttle to jobs.
he and i linger like aristocrats.

i roll over to write this.
his breath brushes the down of my nape.

two friends. in the night our legs
laced and unlaced like sneakers.

our hands clasped
like old ladies' hands.

our sides touched with the humid
smell of a storm approaching.
like a bird flying low
my hand fluttered against his thigh.

Most delightful of all is WILMA ELIZABETH MC DANIEL, an *HL* regular. McDaniel is the "Okie" poet who migrated to California during dust bowl days, and who writes about her people. Like ALFRED STARR HAMILTON she is a largely unacknowledged national treasure; you'll never find her poems in anthologies edited by AL POULIN, JR., DAVE SMITH, ROGER WEINGARTEN, or HELEN VENDLER. Here's McDaniel's "Fronie Has Lost the War":

In light skirmishes
or heavy battle
jewelry has always been your
waterloo
dear dumb-bell Fronie
emeralds certified
genuine soda bottle glass

your ruby earrings
are red gumballs
fluke from a Kiwanis Club
machine

when you dropped your
last two quarters in
and turned the handle
twice

But war is always with us
and you gird up
and move on to other arenas
fake diamond strikes
bonanzas of pure gold
that will turn green tomorrow.

Cheers for *Hanging Loose*.

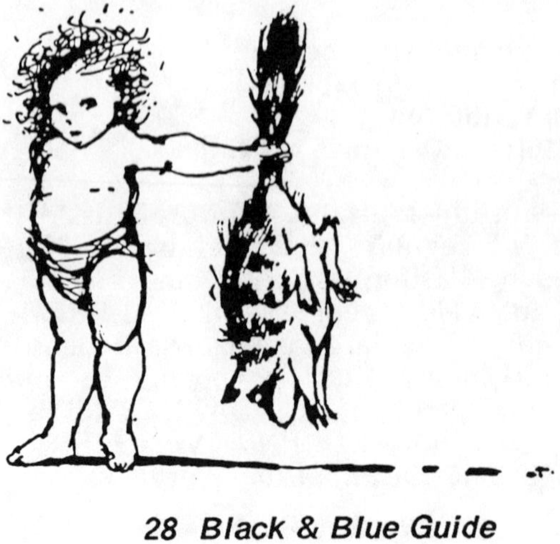

HARPER'S MAGAZINE

Vol. 269: No. 1611 (August 1984). Editor: Lewis H. Lapham. 2 Park Ave., New York NY 10016. Monthly. $18 per year. "Harper's does not publish unsolicited fiction or poetry."

So, if Harper's publishes only solicited poetry why bother to waste space informing poets who might hope to send work there? I review this issue for a section called "Forum," devoted to celebrating the fiftieth birthday of the Academy of American Poets. HENRI COLE, executive director of this hoary body, *cooperated* (this is Harper's word) in seeing this feature through; Cole, it appears, selected these fifteen poems, to tie in with the theme "Naming the Land."

How well do these fifteen poems, by poets both living and dead, reflect a "passion to explore the American text?" The land itself, we are informed, is the text, and the poet's business is "to wrest from the land a separate work of art," whatever that means. The "blank page" confronting the founders of America enabled them to create directly thereon, building houses, cities, a nation. Weren't many of those "pages" smeared with aborigine blood? Like these forebears (these efficient decimators of the Indians), our poets still seek out blank American pages for their scribblings. "Great highways," we are informed, are "still carrying fortune hunters west." As window dressing for the spread of poems this is all pretty insensitive, nay illogical. Even the Academy of American Poets, that ear-trumpet voice of contemporary verse, deserves better. And when the nameless editorial soul who wrote those lines continues, saying that "a filling station or a neighborhood front yard" may occasion a poet's "'greatest poem'," depending on the nature of his details, I want to upchuck. "In front yards, as both WHITMAN and WILLIAMS would have said, there are continents."

Well, how good a mirror of the American space and time-sweep are these poems?

A lengthy "Travels in North America," by WELDON KEES, starts off. Kees trips all over the country (seemingly in no sensible geographical order), staying in motels, watching a "Navajo in levis reading / Sartre in an Avon Pocket Book, against the window / Of a Rexall store," etc. He shivers in St. Paul, bakes in Atlanta, rents a room with brown walls in Boston, observes San Franciso bridges choked with cars and fog, takes a dip in a heated swimming pool in Santa Barbara--but why bore you further? After a page and three-quarters of this meandering, Kees winds up on the Cape and waxes specific: old rafts, spongy two-by-fours, inner tubes, shark spines, crushed codheads, and "two tiny scarlet crabs."

ELIZABETH BISHOP slums, observing an old filling station, run by a soiled, "oil-soaked" father and a couple of "saucy / and greasy sons." The theme is filth: here's her first line--"Oh, but it is dirty." She is happy to see a doily "draping a taboret," and "a big hirsuite begonia." No quiver of feeling here, and when Bishop winds off with "Somebody loves us all," it's enough to send you running to the john. This is "naming the land?" Is this poem really about Bishop's sexual tastes?

In an equally, perhaps even more, insensitive "Enough," MARIANNE MOORE throws her couplets like a gold mesh net over Jamestown, seeking to ensnare all time between 1607-1957. Liver-spots abound: "pests and pestilence" are examples:

found pests and pestilence instead,
the living outnumbered by the dead.

Her insensitive treatment of the Indians is worthy of a child's primer: "Poor Powhatan" and flowering Pocahontas are celebrated in what has to be near-doggerel:

Poor Powhatan
was forced to make peace, embittered man.

Then teaching--insidious recourse--
enhancing Pocahontas, flowered of course

in marriage. John Rolfe fell in love
with her and she--in rank above

what she became--renounced her name
yet found her status not too tame.

Can you believe this? Moore a major American poet? Read your KENNETH REXROTH on this score, folks.

An insipid distancing from the announced theme also characterizes AMY CLAMPITT's "The Cove." She is most genteel, her details placid and comfortable: a "snug house," blue willow patterned plates, whole nutmegs in the spice rack, a nice fire, Mozart, readings of MARIANNE MOORE (ugh), and fond gazings out onto the water where cute little eiders

tuck themselves into the swell, almost
as though diving under the eiderdown
in a *gemütlich* hotel at Innsbruck.

"Upstate," by the trendy DEREK WALCOTT, is full of slack, tired writing. What he says of America, one might say of this poem: "Sometimes I feel sometimes / the Muse is leaving, the Muse is leaving America." Yet, once the lament ends, Walcott sees that its spring, and falls "in love with America." He puts some cold pebbles on his tongue, and, thereby, learns America's "language, / to talk like birch or aspen confidently...." I am sure that old despiser of the pathetic fallacy, SAMUEL JOHNSON is turning in his grave; perhaps so too is DEMOSTHENES.

JAMES MERRILL homes in on the destruction of a

New York City apartment building, one where he once lived. This I don't believe (it's a kitsch observation that sounds true but isn't): "As usual everything in New York, everything is torn down / Before you have had time to care for it." In typically engaging fashion, Merrill tells us what the place, recollected, was like. Everything is in order: TIME is in its place on a table, the walls are "weathering in the general view." At least, the poem is skillfully written, and it should please the more conservative New York City members of the Academy and readers of *The New Yorker Magazine* would tell you, if you asked, what a "good poem" is. Merrill is one of their darlings.

Why CYNTHIA MACDONALD is here, I don't know. Her poem is original, and only tangentially has anything to do with the declared theme of the American land. It's about one girl who has and another girl who has not, on a particular Christmas. It all could just as easily have occurred in France, England, or Spain. The poem remains very personal, with that special mix of personal and public pain Macdonald has made her own.

DOUGLAS CRASE loves the flatulent phrase: "commonplace yards," "to diminish in promise," "borrowed fashions," "mutant enlarging nature." Here are a couple of pompous moments: "when this meeting / Of artifice and artifact occurs, a national monument / Is declared." "How touchingly people embrace the styles / Which look in retrospect like individual good taste." ROBERT LOWELL's sonnet is a mere finger exercise: he writes of a millionaire, a nod, I gather, towards something like having a national level of castes in this mini-anthology. GWENDOLYN BROOKS (is she the token minority female?) sings in the front yard--as distinct from the back yard. Back there the "charity children play." ROBERT HAAS riffs on in prose poetry of no distinction about how Telegraph Hill, Seattle, was not always so steep, and he details the lives of friends who used to explicate EZRA POUND's *Cantos.*

Yes, JULIA MOORE, You Sweet Singer Of Michigan, this gaggle of poems would not be complete without one by the trendiest of all New York poets JOHN ASHBERY. "The Freedom of the House" has nothing at all to do with "America," except that the poet, the house, and the kisses and sighs, and the night (it's "been pushed back again, but cannot say where it has been.") are American.

GJERTRUD SCHNACKENBERG tries to liven up "Elizabeth and Eban, 1940." Details are winsome: the Chocolate Lovelight cake, the fresh coffee, Elizabeth straightening her stocking seams. But the occasional bad line ("The evening steals /Over their windows, as over a pond") suggest that Schnackenberg cared little about this assignment.

ANTHONY HECHT asks BAUDELAIRE's blessing on his mediocre effort, "Birdwatchers of America." He commemorates "a false dusk," soaked steaming hay, and dreams *engendered* by this wandering dusk, brooding "formless and soft beyond the fence." Finally, a cleverish performance by ALFRED CORN begins: "For America is the Garden of /Paradox." Seems like a good place to stop, since Corn's poem, at least, is about clearing wilderness, and the geological vs. the societal age of America.

This *Harper's* feature is a deadend for poets, and delineates more clearly than any critics' ranting or raving what passes for our best writing among minds/members of both *Harper's* and The Academy of American Poets. Perhaps the editors should have sponsored a nation-wide competition, and chosen without any preconditioned ideas. Obviously, the editors didn't care enough to do better, as this mediocre, ill-focused feature shows. It's all a rushed job, yet another indication that poetry counts for very little in prestigious places.

HOME PLANET NEWS

Vol. 5: #2 (spring 1985). Editors: Enid Dame & Donald Lev. POB 415. Peter Stuyvesant Sta. NY, NY 10009. $6 per year.

This newsprint tabloid, now in its 20th issue, continues on its merry way ignoring most of the APR, academic, AWP fat-cat poets and poetesses. The spread is laudably broad: poems, cartoons and drawings, reviews (bordering alas on puffery), letters, translations, and a short piece of fiction. Featured is a not very informative "interview" via letter with CHARLES BUKOWSKI, a somewhat dated "Theater Roundup," enthusiastic reviews of FAYE KICKNOSWAY, ANNE WALDMAN, and EMILIE GLEN. Attention to Glen is particularly welcome, since this poet-madonna of Barrow Street NYC rarely receives her due. The featured poet is NELLIE WONG, who writes poems on topics that count but whose style is as flat as a deflated airmattress. Though a poem by CARL SOLOMON is always news (and good for circulation), his take on madness and "overactivity" is pale. KATHLEEN GRIFFIN supplies a sentimental, vague piece on an "urban nomad." There are some academic exercises--H. PATTERSON writes of Judith and Holofernes, LAYLE SILBERT throws in a so-so found poem based on an editorial by GEORGE STEINER, MARILYN MOHR celebrates Columbus that old "edge of the world" walker. And there's an Ishmael poem by SANDRA WALLER.

One amazing ballad justifies the entire issue: DONALD TUCKER's "The Seventh Rapist," which, according to the note, was "written in prison." An inmate receives his 7th sodomist--this one he loves: "The six took my body, / You're taking my soul."

High marks then for HPN's readability, particularly for its prose. 27 poets appear--most of them unknowns. You'll have a good chance to publish if you're not in the conventional mainstream, are mildly counter-culture, and don't try any fancy verse pyrotechnics or elusive thoughts and images. Much could be done to improve the quality of the verse chosen; the "names" seem to have sent less than their best work--do they fear the newsprint. It does turn yellow fast.

HOW(ever)

Vol I: 4 (May 1984). Editor: Kathleen Fraser. % Jaffer, 871 Corbett, San Francisco CA 94131. $6 for 4 issues.

This is yet another spin-off from the exothermic stuff smothering the Bay Area these days--Language Poetry. Fraser's journal exudes a smugness characteristic of most journals meant for in-groups of whatever gender--her group is women "into" Language.

SUE GANGEL starts off with some doodles (skillful parodies of grade- schooler drawings) with *pomelettes* (they sound like first-draft scribblings) attached. Here's a choice double entendre: "She saw her head out." An image of a "checkered cab" leads to "your de soto hand in mine." I guess we should be grateful that the hand wasn't an Edsel, though De Soto's are today equally antidiluvean. If only Gangel had eschewed pretentious comments about her amateurish art: "I encounter language through visual alphabets, personal hieroglyphs . . . . which plot the action of a shadow rising to from a mirror of itself." Ugh. A good TA instructing bonehead English could help this style a lot.

RAE ARMANTROUT also pontificates ("generally it takes me quite a while to write even a short poem") before treating us to a sample of her versifying. Perhaps if the poems came faster they would be better. She tells us that her stomach is lonely, and that "Heat / did not / come home." What would it be like "if every spurt /left him . . . ."? There's also an Armantrout "Fiction," which reads like undisciplined jottings by a most unhappy woman: "A sense of self starts in the mouth and spreads slowly." Grab the Listerine! This lost soul only LEO BUSCAGLIA could love.

A section of "alerts" follows, where the editors point slim fingers towards "relevant women poets" who have not had their due. RACHEL BLAU DU PLESSIS makes this illuminating comment about SUSAN HOWE: "whole shadow words, as if visual afterimages, come in her intricate split spell-ings: iris sh' (SHDL) or 'life la / nd friend / no lighthous / marin / ere' (CG) . . . ." This is unreadable. One hungers for a clear idea written in simple terms. The greatest intellects--aestheticians, philosophers, and poets have always eschewed darkness visible, darkness inane. What must these *How*(ever) folk talk about when they get together on a rainy day and sip their herb teas? Moreover, I seem to read about SUSAN HOWE everywhere these days. She's neglected?

The poetry of one member of this club, BEVERLY DAHLEN, has interested me for some time. In her most recent book (I've just received a review copy), *A Reading 1-7* (Momo's Press), she is listed as an "associate editor" for *How*(ever). This ambitious new work, ladled out in the form of day-book writing, a form of journalism made fashionable during the height of the women's consciousness movement in the seventies, is greatly marred by the pretentious intellection I have briefly noted above. *A Reading* runs on for some 120 pages, much of it a chore to read. The title itself, numbers in the manner of a latter day LOUIS ZUKOVSKY, hints alas that innumerable parts are due to appear, until the googol is achieved, and Earth's Final Trumpet has sounded.

Orts from all sorts of scattered reading (sometimes assimilated, sometimes not) turn up: WITTGENSTEIN, FOUCAULT, JAKOBSON, DUNCAN, HD, GERTIE STEIN, ROBERT HERRICK, LEWIS CARROLL, NERUDA, FREUD, the old Greeks, the Indian maiden SACAJAWEA, etc. etc.

At one point Dahlen speculates on her being a poet. Note the breathy starts, hesitations, and restarts. Note the solipsistic, almost cute, self-meditation on her self-wonderments. Note the facile symbolism: *key*. Note the trendy furniture of "orgone," and the concealed goddess:

I would not have been a poet.I wonder
why that recurs,I wonder why I
don't think about it.the key.a resistance.key,
Freud knew that even with-
out the censor there would be symbolism.we
cannot speak directly as in
nature,we speak,nature never does,the animal
that makes symbols,tool-
master, weaver,orgone.the man who discovers
her hidden in a tree is . . .

In another passage Dahlen dances along in eurythmic fashion to the stock images of new moon and voodoo doll. I don't much care for the easy association that leads her from "table" to "tabula," or the rhyming "voodoo...wouldn't you," or "chance" and "dance." A few lines further she observes that "All this language is floating." Which seems to have something to do with being different from male writers: "The men make statements. They use the forms of the verb 'to be' with confidence. What I write is provisional. It depends. It is subject to constant modification. It depends."

"Floating" says it: the floating that goes nowhere, and turns back on itself, changing nothing. There's always more talk, always more tea to drink, always more animal innards to read for omens ("you can't tell an omen when you see one," Dahlen writes), always more to think about as you fashion your "critique of pure love," always more bitching to do about a male-dominated society: "a hard pill to swallow. the male bias of psychoanalysis, the male bias of everything, the masculine protest."

And always the revelatory tone, as if some minor priestess of Isis clad in H. D. garb, or ROBERT DUNCAN's drag, is holding forth, swinging the palindromes as if they were censers. Here is an example of the tone at its worst, embodied in the quasi-liturgical mode: "and he/ he who was," "he who is other must be the final mystery, who lives under the law of the dead father," "she who is in the mirror," "she who pondered all these things silently," etc. etc.

Dahlen can be marvellous though when she is not being pretentious, embroidering notes from matters sacerdotal, mythological, psychological, and pan-sexual. Here, for example, she conveys a special urgency; over the years her pain remains undiminished:

Daddy,mom wants you to come home
now,and he bending and turning,
he came,came with me,back.such a man.and
I a child learning the
woman's part,come home now.

And this is first-rate--there's no straining:

there are some plugs like organ stops
which are pushed in and everything
else is going strong.the music honks and it
takes up everything,it is a meal
in itself.

This evocation of a difficult marriage hurts. Dahlen's seemingly simple way of writing, so lyrical and non-hysterical, cuts to the bone:

I suspected he was getting by with a
lot.glowing body,dripping sweat.
there was some backwater I was in,couldn't
get out of it. some slough
where I put myself on again, these clothes.

After she spins off a pretentious Penelope bit inspired by JACQUES DERRIDA's notion of "amor fati," she writes this utterly moving, personal, wise passage:

the reading of the writing goes on,this
is for you because you are not here.
you are always not here.you are never
here.I make you up, I wonder how

you look.and now it is so much easier to write than to speak.an other is so much an hallucination it's scary.I don't know what I speak to.

Certainly, it is not my place to decry the impact of the kind of esthetics extolled by *How*(ever) as a damaging force on a writer with talents as impressive as Dahlen's. I can still recommend *A Reading*, but with the warning that a reader who doesn't love Dahlen straight away, or what she and the Fraser group stand for, will find any concentrated reading difficult, nay, even sleep-inducing. I would love to see the book minus all the intellectualizing, the skimming over concepts which seem so transparent, with all those good passages reflecting Dahlen's own large spirit and personal history.

I have yet to meet anyone who has been able to sit and read GERTRUDE STEIN for more than an hour at a stretch (KENNETH REXROTH alone has had the balls to say so in print), or to remain excited by H.D. after twenty pages or so. These seem the deities behind this sort of writing. A poem is not a dictionary. A poem is not a set of easy metaphysical speculations on the nature of grammar, guilt, or the primal flood. And when Dahlen announces early on that she is "preparing in the most banal way to say everything possible," I shudder. Too true, too true. When I pick up *How*(ever) I shudder. I look "for a line." Nor is facile word play, no matter how "round" and female the concept, poetry: "what in the round, that gave roundness to it, the daily round, it was when I saw the round bowl, the cup, the orange, round, and began it." Let's *not* keep the *trope* flying. Let's strangle the little creature in his crib before he soils his pants and screws up our life. Yes, *How*(ever) people, as Ms. Dahalen says (p. 21): I "know this is a piece of writing."

IMAGES

Vol. 10. No. 3. 1985. Editor: Gary Pacernick. Dept of English, Wright State University. Dayton, OH 45435. Thrice yearly. $3 per year.

Thanks to Gary Pacernick's indefatigable energies *Images* has appeared regularly for ten years. The format is tabloid, on decent paper stock, and is devoted entirely to poems and pictures that celebrate rural life almost to the exclusion of other themes. Here are photographs of tree branches, weeds, a barn door, a hay mow, snow-fence, a dozen eggs, an old gravestone, a farmhouse window, a field, more eggs, etc. The poems match these motifs: birds, a calf, Mrs. Thoreau, dad in coveralls, a frozen dog-corpse, autumn "hills aglow/with October amber," an unused plow.

No single poem or picture could offend a university administrator, a librarian, or a casual reader of verse. Not a single form is experimental. Few poems eschew bucolicism. A sketch of ISADORA DUNCAN, by JOHN DICKSON, rehashes the obvious facts of the dancer's life, with some woeful writing; viz., "out of the cradle endlessly dancing," "suddenly merging from girl to woman," and her children were "drowned like kittens in a sack." JOAN HALPERIN visits Saint-Remy where VAN GOGH lived before he perished: her obsession with the painter's ear doesn't quite make it, nor does her overwriting. HALPERIN shows us Van Gogh in distress at San Remey, as "Bees bang / their furry yellow against its dented mesh [of the painter's hospital cell]." Magical wild roses, "shuttered," now open up, "swallowed cobalt blue." These flowers have "endured the punishment of bees, the mongrel / lapping up its drool." Flowers genuflect and drop their petals. Halperin's device of winding off with an image rather than some sentimental observation on the doomed painter is laudable; too bad her writing isn't up to the challenge.

JOHN TAGLIABUE contributes a pair of political poems designed for a single reading: he's on the right side, but since the writing is generally clumsy (viz., the opening lines of "Dynamic Hardware and The Burning Flesh"), he's not apt to make many converts either to his political ideas or to his verse:

All these motions here there everywhere
going towards the need to make war
objective objective objective
All these motions going towards the need
to make suicide subjective
subjective in the
ward / in the war. Poor distraught
mankind....

There is yet another Homage to SYLVIA PLATH, and an elegy for OSIP MANDELSTAM. The couplets of ELIZABETH BARTLETT's "The Hour of the Wolf," lack both resonant music and idea; it's all most facile, from the inception with a dulled image of life as a "journey," and, as the poem continues, accretions like these: "the farthest reach of the dark," moving shadows, Plath "pursued by tears" as she rushes "down bottomless stairs," trying to escape "fangs and claws." Plath turns into a hissing creature on her knees, feeling (an unfortunate verb) "their drooling howls." Poor thing! "Skin after skin" is ripped from her "nine-layered life."

The writing throughout *Images* is often embarrassing. Here THOMAS SHEEHAN remembers working on a car: "I counted lug nut as coins, / twirled them as doubloons in hand,//screwed them until muscles / told my name, aired my age . . . ." TONY BARNSTONE inhabits a "giant house" which in turn "inhabits" him. Here S. W. BLISS slaps down cliched birds flapping about an "imaginary" landscape. In the one original moment, these obscure birds (crows? gulls? sparrows? shrikes? turkeys?) "bleed their young to sleep." When we are asked to accept these creatures' inner lives, we can't believe it:

Birds soar overhead
dipping,
and flapping.
They cross imaginary borders,
bathing in imaginary pools.
They bleed their young to sleep.
Their inner life keeps silent.

ED OCHESTER concludes a poem with this clumsiness: "and heels walked slowly the iced sidewalks." His "Arvida Klingensmith" is a better rendition of a type of poem special to these journals prizing country matters, the American Gothic Poem:

Every Sunday in nice weather, from the porch
Ed Schreckongost lifts his beercan
in salute as his wife the organist
backs out the old Blazer and growls off
beneath a halo of smoke,
and the oldest parishioner, 103,
is carried in dozing by his great-
grandsons....

SAMUEL MENASHE's sketch of the sea produces a flaccid bit of free-verse doodling, complete with hint of black/white tonality, and this sweet bit: "pen in hand" (penis?):

That black man running
Headlong on the beach
Throws back the white
Soles of his feet
Lightning strikes
Twice on the sand
Left foot and right,
My pen in hand.

J. B. MULLIGAN looks for "light," which he says "is everywhere," beneath rocks, "the dullard skin," and "the brief acts that measure out our lives / in deadened repetition / necessary as a prayer." You may want to add more clichés to his assemblage.

In fairness, there are a couple of passable poems: RAMONA WEEKS' "The Klaeidoscope" and CHARLES WEBB's lean, painful take on a man facing divorce. Once past the triviality of the opening line, and the dull tonality of the journalese setting up stanza two, Webb throws off a poem some cuts above most of the others here:

DIVORCE

I was just scratching my head
when my skull cracked like thin
ice and my hand plunged inside.

I didn't panic, merely pulled out
slowly, to protect my brain.
My hand emerged clutching a wax image

of you. I jabbed my tie-tack
in its gut. Stale gas blasted
my face as the stab-hole ripped wide.

Dusky shapes spewed out, like moths
with foetus-heads. They were
my failures. I knew each by its cry.

My fear is that since *Images* is already ten years old, a rather ripe age for poetry journals, it isn't going to change much. 'Tis a pity.

MID-AMERICAN REVIEW

Vol. IV: 1 & 2 (Spring & Fall 1984). Editor: Robert Early. Poetry Editor: George Looney. 106 Hannah Hall, Dept. of English, Bowling Green State University, Bowling Green OH 43403. Twice yearly. $6 per year.

This ambitious journal reflects the conservatism one would expect of a heartland university. The issues are fat (c. 200 pages), and well-designed. Each issue contains some thirty poems, six good short stories, articles (the best are on SEAMUS HEANEY, JAMES WRIGHT, and "voice"), and some very middling reviews.

One detects the breaths of WILLIAM STAFFORD and JAMES WRIGHT everywhere. Of the sixty-three poems, thirty celebrate family matters dear to heartland America. Nearly the same number feature owls, deer, rabbits, sparrows, and insects. The favorite season is winter: at least a dozen poems are snowbound. Often these themes overlap in a single poem.

JACK DRISCOLL, a poet published by the conservative Ithaca House, writes one of the best pieces on Predictable Themes. "Growing Up With Guns" traces a male's obsession with guns, an obsession he's had from childhood. The setting is bucolic: there are the appropriate animals--horses; there's a nod towards adolescent dancing and sex; a father dies; winter is the season that most matters; the gun helps the lad confront his half-expressed grief over his father's death; and the style is no-nonsense meat-and-potatoes, Iowa Workshop, Experiential, mid-western plain. Here is the entire poem:

There is little time between the crib
and the first pellet entering the bluejay's skull.

I grew up fast,
at twelve clogged the barrel of my air rifle
with a cork,

and from the hip
fired close range at the horse's white face.

BB's came two years later.
I squeezed one in the palm of my right hand
while I slow danced with Brenda Machnic
and my whole body swelled.
I strolled home that night through the
railyard,
stopped and sighted down my empty arms,
imagined a single bullet ripping darkness a
full mile
between the steel tracks.
That winter my father died.
For months I wore his guncase key like a medal
around my neck,
dreamed I unlocked the glass doors
and in St. James Cemetery blasted empty Coke
bottles
above his grave.

Today I am blind in one eye,
not from a richochet,
though that is a lie I tell my son
when I find him wearing my black patch in the
barn.
Squinting down at him
I scare only myself in the familiar half light
of our separate childhoods,
that distance we travel alone with such
imperfect aim.

To the credit of the editors, there are few "names" here. The journal, hence, does a real service to fledgling writers. None of the poems is thoroughly awful, and some are excellent. Among the latter (in addition to JACK DRISCOLL's above) is WALTER MC DONALD--he's the most impressive of the lot. "My Father Quits Another Job" is a memorable Father Recollected Poem. Dad returns from a bar. He's been in a fight, and has scabs of blood on his lips and nose. He's a man of great affections, is frustrated by his job at "that stinking plant" and craves to write. Here's the ending, complete with the ubiquitous snow so prevalent in this journal:

> **Later, his best friend snoring on the couch,**
> **my father gone to his den,**
> **I left him roaring ballads to my mother,**
> **our thin walls throbbing like the gramophone's**
> **dry membrane coming loose. Outside, wet snow**
> **falling fast covered their tracks.**
>
> **I shut my eyes against it. I felt it**
> **puff my face like angel kisses**
> **my father gave once with his lashes**
> **when I came home in tears, holding me tight,**
> **like the heavy coat that seemed now, outside,**
> **the only thing between me and freezing.**

F. KEITH WAHLE writes of a father gone senile who believes he is his son: "'These are my son's pajamas,' he thinks, / taking off his pajamas, 'so I must be my son.'" In TAMIKO LYNCH's "Communion," a strange wife emerges from a lake covered with leeches. ROBERT COOPERMAN's "Van Gogh at the Asylum at Saint-Remy" is a powerful excursion into the painter's memories of a dead brother. He tries to paint that brother; instead his own face emerges, "swallowed in color and bandages, / a pipe in his green mouth, / the lips thick as a body / bloating in the canal."

JOAN COLBY's "Owls" is a nasty, vicious snapshot of life: An owl attacks a boy in a tree, mutilates his cheeks and eyes; another owl appears in the heart of a city, a bird "capable / of looking backwards / to a classic doom"; another owl winters (snow turns up again) in Minnesota near a condo development. Rats, spawned by human civilization, supply provender attracting these owls. Colby hears an infant "screeching" at night, and glances out her window to see the moon swimming "like a great white shark. / The owl hunts alone." There's vintage LAUREL SPEER: "Putting on a Girdle for the Wallace Sterling Tea" memorializes one of those awful generic affairs held at a school prizing itself on sororities and turning out candidates for the marriage mills rather than trained intellects. Here is the poem:

Truly, we didn't think, pulling up elastic and
rubber
with dangling garters, attaching stockings
with seams
and putting on a slip that did not dip below
the hemline
of a hand-knit, mid-calf suit in burgundy or
cool green
any more than we protested shaking the hand of
the President,
standing off in dark suit and tie, freshly
shaved himself
in the afternoon, gripping the flesh of 3000
freshmen.
A handshake was important then and we wouldn't
have thought
to strip off our girdles before the startled
eyes
of black-clad maids putting out crustless
sandwiches
on silver platters. Some girls wore gloves
and my turn
inevitably came. What later seemed important
was the fact
nothing like this could ever happen again.

Finally, for pure form, JIM CUMMINS takes the prize with his "The Perry Mason Sestinas"--marvellous.

THE NEW YORK QUARTERLY

#27(Summer 1985). Editor: William Packard. c/o National Poetry Foundation. 305 Neville Hall, Univ of Maine, Orono 04469. $12 per year. $18 per year for libraries. Manuscripts to NYQ, POB 693, Old Chelsea Sta, NY 10113.

From 1969 to 1979, Bill Packard's *NYQ* was one of the best poetry journals around. The issues had class - the myriad type-faces, the professionalism of the covers, the exceptional quality of the poetry and prose, and the size made it a magazine apart. Only now do we appreciate the efforts required then to keep *NYQ* afloat. To his credit, Bill Packard never allowed a falling off either in the appearance or in the quality of the contents. Included were poets of all schools - BUKOWSKI and STAFFORD, GIOIVANNI and KUNITZ, MC CLURE and SEXTON, DICKEY, and BERRIGAN. There was a healthy mix of known and unknown poets. A valuable feature was the Crafts Interview. These were later collected and published by Doubleday; a new, revised volume is now in the works, via another publisher. Beset by impossible problems - the drying up of contributions and subscriptions, a 350% boost in rent, etc, the journal folded. Only recently has the National Poetry Foundation made re-emergence possible. It's a day for huzzahing!

No. 26 (Spring 85) samples past Crafts Interviews, plus verse held over during the six year hiatus. No. 27, just out, is right on track. There's an Interview with CHARLES BUKOWSKI, one of the best interviews ever by this hoary eminence gris of contemporary poetry. This, one of Bukowski's most perspicacious moments, should chill the spines of Writing Program clones in the country:

"There's too much bad poetry being written today. People just don't know how to write down a simple easy line. It's difficult for them; it's like trying to keep a hard-on while drowning - not many can do it. Bad poetry is caused by people who sit down and think. Now I am going to write a Poem. And it comes out the way the *think* a poem should be. Take a cat. He doesn't think, well, now I'm cat and I'm going to kill this bird. He just does it."

There's an iconoclastic essay by KARL SHAPIRO on the "Present State of American Poetry," the first in a new series of lengthy commentaries by poets invited to hold forth. The satiric thrust is distanced by Shapiro's writing of himself in the third person. Here is "his" over-view of the present state of American verse:

"The downhill speed of American poetry in the last decade has been breathtaking . . . . Poetry plunged out of the classics, out of the modern masters, out of all standards, and plopped into the playpen. There we were entertained with the fecal-buccal carnival of the Naughties and the Uglies [ie., the Beats], who have their own magazines and publishing houses, and the love-lorn alienates, nihilists, disaffiliates who croon or 'rock' their way into the legitimate publishing establishment."

Shapiro is sardonic about his experiences in academe. He goes to John Hopkins as an "Associate Professor with Tenure" - there was "no principle behind it, only a personality." A school for poetry quickly turned into a school *of* poetry, "lines of force sprang into being, attitudes, dogmas, definitions, terms." He is far more scathing re: the University of Iowa School of Creative Writing: there "the new poetics of structure-texture-irony was in full swing"; the atmosphere "got too thick" for "salvaging poets"; there was endless bitterness and backbiting. A "school for salesmen." Poets rushed "to the sow - Iowa is pig-metaphor country - knocking each other over for the choice tit." He is equally devastating on his tenure as editor of *Poetry* during the 'fifties, and on the campus turmoil of the 'sixties.

D. SNODGRASS writes three energetic, lyrically varied, flexible, and keenly felt poems on the theme of

Cock Robin. He provides exactly the playful note BUKOWSKI hopes to see more of in contemporary verse. Here is a brisk rhymed moment from "Cock Robin Takes Refuge in the Storm House." Dig the final end-rhyme:

Like trains colliding, or deep
thunder,
I heard a heavy tree-trunk
buckle,
Crack in the green woods and go
under.
From someplace else, a greasy
chuckle.
They'll need a fourth to play
pinochle.

Here is a passage from the free-verse lyric. Snodgrass's linebreaks and enjambments are uncannily right:

when i set out thistle
seed for finches, i
got thistles, then let
blackcaps and thimbleberries
use up the hayfield's
old manure, let hawthorn and
chokecherry overtop
the rotting orchard.
all song, no doubt,
demands some wilderness, a
little wholesome waste . . . .

AMIRI BARAKA's suite "To Raise the Roof" - six parts are here - fuses poetry and jazz. Is Baraka the same angry person/poet he was in the fifties and sixties? He still has "the urge to kill, the will / to smash what needs smashing . . . / Given the chance / I'll destroy you / capitalism. There / are others / like me." He's best when he moves within a jazz motif:

do it, do it,
you know the old song, sing it sing it
like it never been sung before, like it never
never been sung before, you the one, gon
sing it, so sing it, bay be, sing it, dont
be lame, i need to hear you, and me, and us,
again

By commemorating SCOTT NEARING's 100th birthday, RICHARD EBERHART rehearses for his own. RUTH HERSCHBERGER writes a stirring elegy on the death of a parent: her father turns on the gas, aged 60:

Gas in the anterooms, gas in the den,
Gas on the stairways, gas against the glass,
. . . .
The dead leaf of the living gas,
The dead sill and the living glass,
Pane of forgiveness, sweet at last.
Fast on the pane, and the sill of glass.

LEO CONNELLAN takes a nostalgic look at pole vaulter Don Bragg, whose world record, set in 1942, was toppled only when Fiberglass poles were invented. Bragg's 15 foot mark now seems "little"; to compliment him is like complimenting "an Ice man or an elevator. The Ice man we don't see/ in our electric freezing, Ice man who ran up five flights / with a big block of ice on a rubber mat with water creeping/down it like a blown party favor heavy on his shoulders . . . ." LOLA HASKINS evokes the inner torment of a man (he seems to remain thirteen) who stabbed a best friend with an icepick and claims he poisoned a brother. He fears prison, is

Like a woman waiting for the man
she will fight to the death.
Never knowing when he'll come,
but feeling his approach every moment
in her chest, her teeth, her fingernails.

In STEPHEN STEPANCHEV's "Scars," a woman disrobes, slowly revealing a map of scars on her body... breasts, belly, thighs: she'd been stabbed by a mugger, bitten by a dog, and doused with a pan of hot water by her mom. Stepanchev fingers the scars, kissing each one, eventually marrying the woman: "I distrust all unscarred people." The poem is a paradigm for our lives: how can we get through it without scars? The compassionates (the speaker is one) are the most scarred.

Ten years after serving in the Viet Nam War, ALBERT SANTOLI has become a pacifist. He writes leanly, as if his poem is a letter detailing the war - no fancy pyrotechnics, scintillating leapings and piourettings of fancy image and cadence. He weaves "the whole stinking collage" together "with a belt of .30 caliber machine gun bullets / & fear of exploding L-shaped treelines / at the edge of quiet rice fields."

WING TEK LUM translates a poem about star-gazing into a tender, unsentimental expression of love. DANIEL BERRIGAN, in "Christ Our Lord," addresses his saviour:

you glimmer there in the dark like a
world ransoming pearl -
. . . you
an argument against God's existence
and the jackals chorus -
if he were not

CONSTANCE CARRIER moves through the life of Rebecca Nurse, falsely accused of witchcraft in Salem and hung as a witch. BRYANNE NANFITO's take on neckties is brisk and humorous. The tie is an image for our various trussings corporate and private:

Knots. It must be knots
that keep us together. Tying

TOMB OF UNKNOWN POET

the split. I want your tie,
your necktie to lead me by,
going through hell.

Far more ambitious and complex is ANDREW GLAZE's "Acrobats," a poem deserving several readings. Acrobats traditionally give faith "*to nothing*," and "spit upside down at the absolute." Acrobat-poet joins the clowns:

Difficult, backward crabs, they come here to me
- friendly - such honks of vegetable noses!
Poor crippled carrots, waggy artichokes,
rotten hand-sewn idiot baggy pants.
Which is my squint? What leers down my owlish
cheeks?

WILLIAM STAFFORD has a cute lyric about his poems snatched up from a river by an eagle: now, somewhere in a forest, its pages turned by the wind, the book educates eagles. ROBERT LAX writes a one-syllable per line bit called "Spider," meant, I guess, to look like a spider's thread spun through the white air of these pages. Not much, for me at least, latches in.

MAY SARTON is pretentious about carnage in a road: the moral? "Destructive man, poor rat, just keeps on going." ANDY CLAUSEN's "Soldiers of Christ" is a devastating look at a Marine Corps base on Sunday when all the men are expected to attend worship services. Drill Sergeant, via "a short swift deep shot" to an "atheist's breadbasket," sends the latter off saying he's a Protestant. Read this poem along side E. E. CUMMINGS's "I sing of Olaf."

In DAVID COPE's "Modern Art," a street bum on a street corner during rush hour has it his way. CHRIS BROWN's "Blackfoot" is a somnolent hymn to the Indian "opus of the Great Flow: slow meridian of the act." STEVE KOWIT expands amusingly on a rumor that after Watergate NIXON, incarcerated for good in a mental institution run by Quakers, was replaced by the CIA with a double. Pat prefers the double:

It was only at night, on the springs,
that she had to admit that his flashy, showbiz
routines
were a hundred precent more entertaining
than Dick ever was
with his shrill little whines & patsy caresses
& miniscule twanger.

BILL DURHAM's rodeo rider is clobbered by a Brahma bull, is hospitalized, tries for the purse, and fails again. Durham has starch and energy:

He bucks and spins
and you stay hard in the
saddle pitching, spurring,
thinking oh, his name is
so goddamned true, and as the
sixth second ticks by
you feel the saddle slip
even before the far-away pop
of the cinch you should
have replaced last season.

PATRICIA O'CALLAGHAN translates GUILLAUME APOLLINAIRE's "Sante Prison": "How bored I am between bare walls / Painted pale colors / A fly on the paper with little steps / Wanders across my uneven lines . . . ." CAROL PURDY's poem on the moon and a lover is better graphics than verse. I'll remember PAT SMYKLO's "Agnew State Mental Hospital 1971" a long time; she's in a room with thirty other women, she's naked, seeks "another Jew" to enfold in her arms, so as to "heal" herself. JOAN SHAPIRO's "Gluttony" is a clever throw-away (throw-up-away): a women eats brie cheese while driving, at 3 a.m., loses control of her car, and dies with the cheese stuck in her throat: "but that's / not what / killed her." STEPHEN LUPACK's "Left Behind" forces itself on us without any particular winsomeness: I don't much care about the person Ulysses abandoned on his travels, especially when he speaks these dull phrases: "reduced to insignificance," "pools of incredible darkness," "unspeakable giants." Why, when American poets write on Ancient Themes do they write so pretentiously? Is that their image of how those Greeks talked to one another? "Towers of flesh," indeed!

Now, on the other hand, JAMES MC GLYN eschews that sort of writing. I prefer it to "Left Behind" any day.

Tie large dead animal to rear fender
& drag past house of girl
you wish to impress - honking horn.

Some 90% of the poems in this *NYQ:27* are worth reading and re-reading. That's a rare ratio for any magazine. How does editor Packard come up with so much high-level work? Does *NYQ* simply receive only the best work from contributing poets who respect the magazine enough not to send their stuff there. Why, by contrast, are *Poetry, The American Poetry Review,* and *The Iowa Review* so lacking? Certainly, the reputation for quality nourished by the earlier ten-year run of *NYQ* helps. Kudos go to Packard for his eclectic tastes, and for eschewing coteries. Poets of all persuasions have a chance here, both those who are already known and those who aren't. And Packard's own contributions are unique: he'll include a modest poem of his own, provide a feisty and iconoclastic editorial on aspects of current poetry, and write an hilarious appendix of put-on ads, "personals," and "services" notices. Here is a sampling of these:

Applications are now being accepted by NEA for the most unknown poet you know. Winner will be stuffed in canvas sack and buried in National Cemetery where honor guard will fire couplets over his or her remains, visiting dignitaries will lay decaying laurel wreaths on grave as marine bloodhounds will bay at moon.

Isn't that a delicious take on recent obsessions with that absurd Poet's Corner in St. John the Divine, or the dumb formalizing of a Poet Laureateship by Congress? Both represent a further lamentable sanitizing of American verse, honoring what is utterly safe and dead.

This "Personal" lovingly flirts with bad taste:

Surrogate mothers wanted to implant poem embryos until they reach full term, we pay monthly stipends, provide food allowance for mother. ATHENA LABS, Hoboken, NY.

And this:

NATIONWIDE AIRLINES announces 35% group discount for state poetry societies flying to annual meetings, also special rate for ejecting undesirable poets from altitude of 30,000', $350 per poet.

This, by way of warning:

My wife, Amanda Honeyfeather, having left my bed and board and having persisted in writing about me in her poetry, I am no longer responsible for any disturbances that may take place during her poetry readings. Augustus Honeyfeather.

And this should indeed inspire the NEA to withdraw all funding for Poets in the Schools programs:

PARAKEET POETRY READINGS
The National Endowment has announced sponsorship on state level for all talking parakeets that have not previously given poetry readings. Birds will be sent into kindergarten where they will chirp monosyllable poems to pre-schoolers. Applications must be on file no later than September 27, must include name of bird, sample tailfeather. All states eligible except New Hampshire which doesn't go along with any of our more innovative projects. $5000 per bird, plus bird seed, change of gravel.

NYQ belongs in all libraries, in living room magazine piles, and in the bathrooms of all poets and critics who wish to keep au courant with the today's best writing.

ORIGIN

5th Series: No. 4 (Fall 1984). Editor: Cid Corman, with assistance from Michael Heller, George Evans, Sherman Paul, Gil Ott, Lyle Glazier, Theodore Enslin, et al. 2 or 3 times per year. Box 981, Stuyvestant Station, NY NY 10009. $12.

This handsome journal, judging from this issue, is a closed shop. Of the ten featured writers, only two are not on the masthead. In the past, Corman has been an eclectic editor, showcasing poets not in his stable of consultants and associate editors. Whether this issue heralds a shift remains to be seen. I shall examine only this particular number.

Corman blasts MICHAEL RIFFATERRE's *Semiotics of Poetry* (Methuen, 1980), calling his piece "Semi-Idiotics." There's a winsomeness in Corman's naivete - I assume it's a put on: "Insofar as I can grasp what is called 'semiotics' - a word that began circulating early in the century in linguistic circles - it deals with the general theory of the modes of signifying . . . . No wonder - indeed - that poetry baffles most wouldbe readers. They are systematically encouraged to be baffled." The Professor's "twists and turns and endless 'allusions'" are beside the point. Riffaterre "is a pedant - but half his pedantry derives from his wizardry at utilizing dictionaries . . . . He often uses texts that are gratuitously boring - even by his own admission . . . . He develops fancy names for elements that have been grasped at least as far back as ARISTOTLE." And so on and so on. The piece is a corrective to the J. HILLIS MILLERS and JACQUES DERRIDAS of the current academic world, and their hosts of followers. The sad fact is, alas, that Corman/*Origin* won't be read where it counts. Corman rings in with "Peace," as DAVE GARROWAY used to do - Corman calls him "Galloway." Finally, the editor's own efforts to illuminate LOUIS ZUKOVSKY are as arcane and mindscrewing as anything Riffaterre writes. Here's just one example:

The word "hoe" (with its semblance to "ho" and "O") calls out/evokes "money" and "sunday . . . joe" echoes "Sancte Iohannes."

Or this:

The quincunctial structure - 5 words per line and 5 lines for the poem - would - if 80 TREES may be taken as a sign (and I think it may) - have been retained throughout -- religiously.

Editor THEODORE ENSLIN contributes a pallid prose piece on the heirlooms he's acquired. His "5 Poems" read like doodlings in the dust on old grandad's escritoire. Here's an example:

A Sheraton highboy - always my father's. I never appreciated it until I had it. The nine drawers *are* shallow. But they are adequate, and clothes, once spread out, easier to find than in deep drawers. It was the first Theodore's, my grandfather. I thought it might be a reproduction, until the estate appraisers assured me it was not.

MARK RUDMAN contributes four skillful poems inspired by self-isolation, as Nature carries on with rain-storms, thunderclaps, sea-tides. Rudman is a new Adam naming objects. He accepts (and here he lets me down): "What is. And is about to be." Here, he sings the pain "of numbness":

No longer to ponder the morbid denials,
I will mourn, break down the sentimental,
human distinction of age,
embrace this death no one escapes.

Let the fire rage.
Let these ashes stand for life -
raw, unkempt, nervous -
like a friend who claims she has been numb for
months,
in one kind of pain if not another.

More nature riffs from editor GEORGE EVANS: banging screen door, ice cream, frog legs, an old house - all it's history going, gone gone. Here he considers the anonymity of ants:

The ant line streams both ways,
a river with two currents.

Yes, I'm stupid & fight the flow.
This one crawls by with a comrade,

this one a twig, crumb & sugar bearers
meet then go on. Yes I am stubborn

persnickety & rude. They pass on the wall
or porch or street loving the feel

of each other, letting daddy-longlegs
cross their line headed for light.

I know I'm small & nothing will happen
beyond limits of the universe . . . .

In another of his poems he's on a drive, stops to change a flat, complain, and "piss." He sees meditational value in a crushed napkin, a dark circle of coffee, a dead bunny beside a road. His fascination with the mundane grows mundane and precious:

I count the grains of stone in the wall
without looking at the wall.
Somewhere my feet walk through a meadow
in the small dream, of a grasshopper.

True, he's writing here of a prisoner - and here's a definition for forthcoming dictionaries: "Terror is sitting / in one's own piss." Yet, his rampant solipsism elsewhere makes it difficult to read "The Prisoner" as anything but yet another poem about Evans himself.

Britisher CRAIG WATSON loves the hollow abstractions British poets persist in loving: "endlessness," "sacrifice," "spirit," "an inherent discipline to gravity." And he layers his lines so that lots of white is visible between each, as though each line is a koan. Boring! boring! Here Watson jots pompous observations. The echo of *near* in *hunger* is woeful:

DISSOLVE

Resist dual voice.

Feel endlessness survives,

one day, two,

the promise to sacrifice half-mask.

Always spirit chooses hunger.

In chasmic streams a longing hung;

and rain torques away the lines of near.

Featured poet LYLE GLAZIER presents twenty-six pages of an on-going autobiographical poem "Azubah Nye." Azubah, an Indian maid, married Glazier's great-great grandfather. Time telescopes - Glazier is as much preoccupied with his immediate life as with his ancestors. What ties them together is Nature (all poets in *Origin* share this), self-reliance (there are passages on a grandfather's sawmill), and marginal flirtings with homosexual feelings (another boy uses Glazier's six-year-old thighs for intercrural sex). "The spirit of the mountain / infected my spirit," Glazier writes. This flaccid observation might better have been edited out. Glazier has a penchant for dull passages of reportage, viz:

when for the first time
in more than fifty years
I slept again in the little
bedroom off the entry
in the old house
the valley house, tired
by a drive from the Cape

Snore, snore.

When Azubah has sex with Glazier's blonde ancestor, one has the feeling that Glazier is himself quite turned-on, perhaps translating himself into a Rima-figure. The risk he takes is that when he writes of a primitive, he writes primitively, with a Dick and Jane simplicity: "He saw you lurking / knew you were there, / made plans for evening / after work was done . . . ." Here he does less than justice to his dying grandmother: "Gram dead from hawking her lungs out / in the northwest bedroom, / I gave her a clean rag / to spit into . . . ." His best writing is understated. Here a man loses an arm in a sawmill accident:

a saw leaped and
rid him of one arm
above the elbow . . .
The shrill of the saw
sent tremors along my nerves
though the smell of sawdust
excites my nostrils still . . . .

Here, the language turns magical:

I hear the click
of trennel in the hand-forged latch
of the flimsy door
on the stairs
between pantry and kitchen . . . .

Unfortunately, there simply isn't enough of this kind of writing. Here he's dull and sentimental: "Gramp loved the woods, / he walked his boundaries / once a year / on his birthday . . . ." There are the "right" ecology sentiments - ravishing the forests, polluting the streams, etc. In an earlier assessment of this poem in progress (*The Small Press Review*, Feb. 1985) I was more enthusiastic than I am now. Glazier's simplistic writing seems now contrived and postured.

Corman appears to seek out wan poets who write with pallor, who assume that commonplace thoughts, observations of nature, and ancestries recollected generate meanings like those of that one hand clapping, that pine tree falling in the forest with no ears around to hear it, or that chicadee poised on a flowering plum branch in snow.

The latter has beauty, certainly. But these poem orts don't: "Screen door bangs gravel leaps / car spins out" (EVANS); "That was after / Pop had his job / in the stockroom" (GLAZIER); "If I trace silence / some will say I trace nothing. / But what I trace has substance, / other, more than, //dust" (ENSLIN); "The trees know this. / The wind soughing in the trees knows this" (RUDMAN). Glazier might profit from DONALD JUNKINS' *The Agamenticus Poems* (Hollow Springs Press, 1984) which treats material from a similar past far more imaginatively and energetically. Corman himself, in a riff printed inside the front cover, entitled "The Community of Individuals," delineates the problem: "Reality is brought to mind by the inadequacy of any statement of it, the tension of that inadequacy, the direction and force of that statement." The conclusion? Keep silence. And if thou must speak, thou shalt not bore thy readers!

OUTLAW

4 & 5: 1984 Editor: David Spicer. 323 Hodges St., Memphis TN 38222. An "Irregular anarchic journal devoted to anything the editor deems unworthy of publication elsewhere." Single copies $2.50. Subscriptions $10.

In THE PETERS BLACK AND BLUE GUIDE: SECOND SERIES, I wrote critically of *Yellow Silk*, a journal featuring "erotic" work. I found it much too tame. I recommended that the editors take a look at *Fag Rag* as a daring "erotic" lit mag. I wish I had known then of *Outlaw* - I would have also recommended it. Poems and prose pieces here reek eroticism. Some are kinky and absurd, with generous political overtones. There are several delicious nose-thumbings, fart-blastings, cunny-linguistings at the political and literary establishments. RON ANDROLA celebrates a wife's *tabu* scented privates. COREY MESLER reports a blow job given by "an angel" who flies off to Texas "to help the poor." LYN LIFSHIN's "Stripper Madonna" has a tongue that flops out, resembling a boa; she behaves as a turn-on by flicking her g string, spreading her buttocks in a mirror ("melons the round / musky kind)," and masturbating. SETH WADE's man with an artificial left hand has more than his share of women. He worries about his anal warts and poetry: anal and penis warts, he boasts, make him "more interesting" to the ladies . . . "old age that adds / as it takes away." Flat-breasted poetess Cora Bess Quackenbush is his competititon: no matter how many sex poems she writes she'll never be sexy to him. S. K. MORGAN boasts of being "the weird, crazy, perverted one": like most of the poets here he's casual, almost diffident, which comes off as pretentiousness:

> **hell, i just write poetry**
> **talk of the right and mostly wrong**
> **in this manic, fucked-up world**

and you say i'm strange?

in your ear, asshole
go play with yourself in traffic . . .

Reading PETER BRETT's "151" is a relief; here's one poem that has something more than skid-mark verse, delayed teen-ager dirty-talk poems. Mexican Paco gives brother Juan 151 silver dollars, to assist him on his way to California. Juan succeeds as real estate entrepreneur, and never honors his debt to his brother. One Christmas, Paco sends him 151 hot green peppers; eventually, Paco receives a deed for 151 acres of land.

Back to the trivial: JIM HEYNEN writes of a farmer who won't have an indoor toilet: "Not even a dog shits in his own house." And his bit on the woman who keeps pink curlers in her hair to dissuade men from her beaty, is thoroughly forgettable.

MARKESAN MORRISON writes the poem to end all poems on the automobile as a sex object: "Mazda Love" is delicious. The energy outmatches the slack writing, and he can't resist the impulse for sleaze - he's a better poet than that - something he doesn't seem to know. Who cares that he wants "to eat peppermint-pussy / Ice cream at Ho-Jo's?" Here's a better moment:

I'm longing for bug-smear
On the windshield, on the fender smiling
Sullenly matte black; a little tar on the
Wheel-wells, a little bird-doo on the
Curving phallic hood, dust in the eyes
Under their lazy silver lids;
Road-dirt to deflower this Hero,
This snaking cat of the road
Who has taken its shape.

The most visible poet is SESSHU FOSTER who writes a long 10 part poem about Los Angeles. TODD

MOORE is the only other poet approaching him for quality. "Lines in Red & White for L. A." is a pastiche of love/hate. Here is #8:

**The smell of waiting in Los Angeles
is most often noticed at bus stops
or riding the bus in crowds battered
by old men who sleep in their clothes.
It drifts from streets where broken down
cars and broken glass glitter in wait
for the children to come home from school and play.**

**It is in the life of eroded, empty lots.
It could be most characterized by the wrinkled
old man who stood in guaraches, soles
cut of tire treads in the dust now wearing
tennis shoes from South Korea and watching
the traffic for a chance to cross the street.
Next to him the dog run over and lying corrupt
beside the freeway onramp smells less
of waiting.**

The fiction is nearly always outrageous: RODNEY C. MURRAY's Bert Pickle has a sore penis that won't quit. He's befriended by a bum who lives as a slave behind a bar. The bum's dick has rotted off. In L. CIRINO's stunning "Biscayne" a trapeze artist and his daughter (his wife died in a fall from the ropes) perform naked, fucking, then fall to their deaths.

Outlaw is not for everybody. It's mimeographed format is these days a welcome rarity. Spicer also publishes a glossy journal *Raccoon,* much more conservative in its tastes than *Outlaw*. The latter is to the former as *Playboy* is to *The New Yorker;* one you tuck out of sight when the priest comes to dinner; the other you display on the fumed oak coffee table. Another difference: you need not write as well for *Outlaw* as for *Raccoon*. I guess we need the occasional journal which allows poets to get their rocks off on the page instead of on lavatory walls. One hopes that the eventual effect is a broadening of tastes away from the conventional norms of sanitized language and themes. *Outlaw* despite its flaws is good reading.

Addendum: I find that I happen to have *Outlaw 3* in hand, and so will see what goes on their, briefly. Some of the same poets appear: LIGI (Editor's note: Ligi "has hooks instead of hands." He writes "disgusting crap"); LAURENCE HARGRAVE ("a biker serving a stretch in the Maryland Can." His poems are typed "as is, mispellings and all, to illustrate the crude genius . . . .'"); TOOD MORE (says ye. ed: he's "slicker than I am."); SETH WADE ("lives down in Texas, where farts are quite common"); TOM HOUSE (he's "probably as skinny as his poems"); DALLAS WIEBE ("one nasty-mouthed individual. He must have tenure.")

Among the new nasties are surprise, surprise, AL POULIN, JR., of Boa Books, translator of RILKE, and ring-master of a most successful academic poetry anthology. Here's Spicer's toadying note: "A. POULIN, JR. is one of those M.F.A. Babies who doesn't take himself too seriously. Congratulations, Cock Man."

Well, what are Cock Man's poems like? In one his cock becomes a morning crower. The transformation occurs after a good drunk, when poet, clothed, sleeps the night away in a barnyard. His face (the sun comes up) is "a pink pig's, / my toes chicks scratching in the grass." The wind off? A purple passage on his purple-shafted cock:

Purple necked, plumed gold and red
in the blazing sun, perched
on the fence of my open zipper,
my cock crowed and crowed and crowed.

The second Al Poulin, Jr. Poem has this amazing title: "Reading Proust, Or, A Pig At Heart, The Poet Fantasizes That He Is The Angel of Roses." Sounds more like tame GENET, rather than PROUST, doesn't it? Again, the drift is masturbatory and cock-self-congratulatory:

My sperm is like a whale's,
distilled. I could've made
a fortune selling it to Avon.

His cock is, folks, "deodorant in a spray can." Why? Because "it comes so sweet." He "comes" all manner of good things: "a steepled hayloft," a lilac-filled bowling alley, a valley full of "lilies of the valley." The culmination? He *coaxes* his cock to spurt forth a dozen long-stemmed roses, "one at a time." Be warned! You'll never know under which woodpile our most conservative lit czars, publishers of Pulitzer-winning vols. of poems, sedate translators, may be hiding.

PETER WILD seems out of place here: no sick farts, no aromatic (and other) jackings-off, no penis admirations, no sour-grapes attacks on academics, no "I'm Sick Of Life Poems" (viz, LIGI's subtle observation: "if I kill myself it's gonna be / I had enough this shit"), no gangsters or murderers - just plain poetry of the sort Wild writes. More in tune with *Outlaw*'s drift is HAL J. DANIEL III's "Bogata": it reads like a companion piece for Poulin's penis-obsession, though HJD is nastier:

Sleeping with her
was like sleeping
with a pig
on a rotisserie.
Her hot, greasy
swollen body rotated
counter-clockwise
over and over
all night long.

Nuff said! Grunt! Grunt!

THE PIKESTAFF FORUM

(#5, Spring 1983). Editors: Robert D. Sutherland and James R. Scrimgeour. Box 127. Normal, IL 61761. 40 tabloid newsprint pages. Annual. $10 for 6 issues.

60 poems, 39 poets, and 1 translator (of 7 poems by CHARLES BAUDELAIRE) in this issue. A pretty hefty gaggle. The editors' announced preference for poems of "lived experience" does at once set immediate limits: no experimentations, no personas. The Ego Poem (the *I do this I do that* Poem) abounds. Rusticity also abounds. Implicit are various norms for subject matter and diction: you'll find no four-letter words, no detailings of violence (the religion of our times), no specific sex, few words that an intelligent high school graduate from an average midwestern town would not know. Grandma (and there are poems to her) would not be offended, unless a wasp swung over and left his droppings on the old dear's spectacles, as she was reading.

Many poems are forgettable fillers - short wingless things that dip their beaks in tepid milk and skim away. One of these, by MARYBELLE CAMPBELL celebrates the flight of eight pelicans. There's no way, either biologically or metaphorically, that the wings of a pelican in flight could ever resemble waving kite tails.

DEBRA KAY VEST's "The Extra" has a nice proletarian touch (she seems to love the sleeping worker), although her verbs are asked to carry too much freight:

> **Sunlight plows the road.**
> **Dust explodes into sparrows.**
> **Let the worker sleep.**

Beginnings are too often mundane and lassitudinous: "In truck-stop restrooms by the Interstate," "She worked / at the library / downtown," "Now that the ticket is in my wallet," "It's raining again." "Talk like a human being." These are random examples. Here, poor grammar seems intended to put the not too literate reader at ease: "Me and my friends like summer and baseball games."

Here's a sampling of interests: cows, coots, grandma putting on her shoes, father staring at grandma's false teeth in a glass by her bed ("her teeth refuse to speak"), a poet mourning a dying old father whilst sitting in a rocking chair on the front porch at evening (dad's upstairs, "a cricket/ caught in a skeleton's ribs"),an interminable meditation on a pinecone in the manner of ROBERT BLY's meditation on a chunk of wood riddled by ants and termites, nostalgia bits on days when movies were cheap and there was no TV, easy allusions to LORCA and POUND, a "naked" stroll "through your wilderness," blackberries, red-checked apron, and on and on.

90% of these poems fail to rise above the commonplace either in insight or style. Typical is the two or three word line repeated, like the Chinese water torture treatment - the monotony eventually drives you crazy. TOM HOUSE's "Coming Out" employs such lines - they have the life of a somnolent snake stuffed with a freshly-swallowed piglet. In addition, House coyly spins cliché's on their heads, hoping to find honey amidst the brambles:

the meek can
have the earth
(they deserve it)

laughter burst from my
mouth without
benefit of brain

we are all equal
only some of us less so

too long have my rod

and my staff
they comforted me
. . . .

DEBRA KAY VEST, in "Pine Cone and Variations : for Robert Bly," has trouble generating her ambitious tri-partite meditation. She first avers that the cone resembles "the stretched neck of a wild turkey / whose head was severed and burned last November." The pine seeds are the birds "stiff wooden feathers." This just doesn't work, and when in the curving spine of the cone Vest espies "the memory of a hestitant cleaver," I run off to the woods to contemplate my navel. Why is the cleaver "hesitant?" Sure, because whoever was about to whack the gobbler's head off was hesitant. Vest's ill-felt, arty way turns me off. Cone-pitch = congealed turkey blood? She's reminded "of bath oil, Christmas/candles, the hoof of a deer sunk in rotting mulch."

She misses the point entirely of BLY's superb poem - everything fits there - there's nothing forced; and, shortly, when Vest tells us that her dad "was a pine cone stolen from under boughs/of a small town," I'm embarrassed. When she spins the cone "round and round," hoping for quasi-mystical moments, the best she can do is observe a scrambling, emergent insect with spastic antennae and hairy legs. Her comment: "It is an eye which looks out/of the petrified body and sees itself." I'm still trying to see a body petrified (is it her father's?) with an eye (where is the other one) seeing itself? I am relieved when Vest turns the poem on herself, asking this woeful question: "Is my brain a pine cone?" We can't hold Bly responsible for this poem!

I'd like to try an experiment. Here are some lines. Who wrote them? One poet or many?

1

After they leave, I slip under my office door . . . .

2

I admit
I always wanted to slip
an ace from my sleeve . . . .

3

we stand at the pond
reflecting on each other, upon the winter-water

4

late at night
when my beautiful wife
is asleep
i wander away from the television set
go back to my desk
pick up my book of poems
accepted and published . . . .

I could go on, assembling passage after passage written in casual free verse forms, without capitals, with much enervation in the chopped up lines (most are really prose). Yes, each of the passages is by a different writer.

The good poem is rare. One is MALCOLM GLASS's "Building," in which a man builds his own coffin and then climbs in and lowers the lid. True, the "I"s he lavishes throughout assume the look of rye kernels in cowflops. And he is unabashadly casual, developing the details of his carpentry with incredible slowness; he's a tedious old fart proud of his skills: "This/is work I would show anyone." At this point we don't quite know what he's up to. Here are the closing lines:

I turn
the brass screws in on soap below
flush, deep in counter-sunk holes,
fill them over and sand with four-
hundred paper. I want to hide all signs
of joining even from my own eyes
and fingertips. With emery cloth
I wear away a little bowl in the
bottom - a place to rest my head.
Then I lie down in this inland ark.
The smell of wood sanded but unfinished
is a comfort I had not counted on
I turn my head and listen to the hairs
on the back of my skull rubbing against
themselves like rolling Australian pine
needles between thumb and fingers.
The strength of this haven suits me.
My shoulders barely touch the sides,
my toes just reach the footboard.
I lower the lid and see the precise
fit as it blocks out all light
at once. I know the work is
not perfect, but it's as close
as I can get this time.

There's absolutely no straining here, and the tediousness of the carpenter's voice underlines the irony of the whole event, self-burial.

I want to like ROBERT JOE STOUT's "The Coot," and do, much, until he lets me down. The sad bird is caught in a pigeon snare and "flaps into flight" dragging wire and a chunk of two-by-four with it. The wood *ploughs* the lake-water. Finally, the bird tires, dives, and the wood goes under. Surfacing, the coot returns to shore, dragging the float, where perplexed it sits "sharpening its bill on the wetted wood." Somehow, to tell me that the wood is wet is gratuitious, as is the final image of the bird on the beach crouching and blinking.

Another good poem is KENNETH POBO's "Aaron

Sees a Ghost." A youth bored with his job checks guests at a Glen Ellyn Holiday Inn:

On each floor, the same
magazine heads, the same cartlike bodies.
. . .
All the Art in DuPage County
can't reflect
the boredom of coffee tables,
the deafness of lamps . . .

Mermaids that might make the place magical are missing. Aaron feels a haunting kinship with arriving, weary guests, and

feels
the sympathy of one who has touched
naked flesh
and felt bare bone . . . .

He seems wise in his aging, and juggles private images of mermaids singing in appletrees with shadowy, grey-suited men demanding the steak dinner "at the end of the rainbow." Aaron sees the ghosts.

In JUDSON JEROME's *Poet's Market 1986* the editors of *Pikestaff* claim they receive around 3,000 submissions per year, and that they publish 3% of that. I can't believe that the rejected pieces are much worse than most that appear here. One does welcome *Pikestaff*'s energy - they publish some fiction (very short), prose poems, feature young writers (as young as 10), have a section of opinion supplied by readers, a few reviews, and profiles of editors of other literary journals. The format (17 3/4" x 11"), on cheap newsprint, does not make for easy reading. The graphics are humorous bits from old journals and books, the photos are unremittingly bucolic - snow-covered trees, a rural church, an abandoned house. But, judging from this issue (and another recent one) the editors seek few risks whatsoever, and poets thinking of sending work are advised to submit easy-read, free-verse, direct experience poems. In their favor, the editors devote much space to unknown writers. There is no evidence of an in-house coterie at work, slurping up the pages.

PLANET DETROIT MAGAZINE

(#7, 1986). Editor: Kurt Nimmo. Box 28414. Detroit MI 48228. 56 pp. $8 per year, includes chapbooks (current titles: CHARLES BUKOWSKI's *Relentless As the Tarantula* and STEVE RICHMOND's *Gagaku*). The chapbooks may be ordered separately for $2.50.

Much venom flows through *Planet Detroit Magazine*. CHARLES BUKOWSKI and STEVE RICHMOND are featured. Richmond, that much under-appreciated Los Angeles poet, speaks for most of these writers, proud of their proletarianism, and their Newsweekly, non-academic, street-wise proccupations:

> **this poetry writing is my punching bag**
> **lowell and edmund wilson and t s elliot (sic)**
> **would have this be more**
> **but their work doesn't excite me**

One suspects that Richmond adds the extra "l" to TSE's name on purpose, to irritate any conservative poetry buffs who might read his chapbook.

DAVID COPE, D. H. LLOYD and JOHN ELSBERG scribble the "Newsweek" or "News of the Day" Poem. Lloyd rejects Reagan's boast that the air of America is cleaner than ever. Cope reviews events seemingly read from the nightly news, and takes comfort in a sentimental image of "Hoagy's tired eyes," which dates Cope: my guess is that no reader under forty would get the allusion, unless they've seen that old Carmichael/Bogart film. Even LYN LIFSHIN contributes a mediocre Current Events poem (is there any topic she can't write up, on demand?), "When Jesse Helms Buys CBS."

The Immanent Destruction of the Universe obsesses these poets. To S. K. MORGAN humans are a "zillion of thumb-sized / toads hopping about / minding their own damn business" sets up for the big boom, and the resulting fallout of "nuclear starling shit." JOE MACK strolls along singing about detonators so delicate a feather can set them off. There are also poems about being busted and jailed, and several about junk and dope. There are also sex poems, usually of male failure. Here's CHRISTINE LAHEY-DOLEGA's "typical male":

helpless, engorged, and battered
by winds of sex like a weathercock

and with no choice but to register
passing fancies in that privy spot

where the root threatens to,
nay, finally does, burst the seams.

Antidotes for coping with such a hostile world? Smear graffitti on the Poem World Walls, then burrow down in the manner of an earlier idol, the secretive novelist B. TRAVEN. Smear snot, merde, and blood on walls, all the while shouting your pain: "bullshit bullshit bullshit" or "Merry Christmas my ass" - both shouts here delivered by JIM DANIELS. EDDIE VAN HORN wipes both snot and spit off the walls. A. D. WINANS takes a cheap shot at a former friend who hits big enough with a novel to afford "lavender toilet paper." Does old prole Winans use no paper at all?

When these Poems of Reportage and Immediacy work best, they transcend the limitations of the throwaway riff. DAVID COPE's "Antietam" is one of the best. He travels with a woman past the famous Civil War site. She notes the modern transformations of this hallowed spot where thousands of young men died:

in the cornfield where the blue boys lurched &
shrieked,
the canons're set up as in the old photograph,
but freshly painted, with an asphalt walkway curving
around.

& in Bloody Lane, where bodies were heaped up
waist high,
I marvelled at bees in the corn tassles not 30 feet
away.
at Burnsides Bridge, the lazy river barely
rippled.

V. E. STEINHOFF's "Nick Had A Dress Leather" commemorates lost youth and shares with many *Planet Detroit* writers a hard-boiled narrative poem (I've elsewhere called these BUKOWSKI Gab Poems). Friend Nick, had a great leather jacket suitable for hiding bottles of screwdrivers stolen from liquor stores. The drunk that ensued, the charades of pulling knives on one another and the world, prompts "mother," that horrid old gash, to call the cops.

One of the best writers of the Hard-Boiled Mode is TODD MOORE who contributes two poems, written in his customary taut-eared lines. In "Driving Past," a kid bites off the head of an aerosol can, sees Moore watching, puts the can between his legs, and pretends to "jack it off." A more rewarding poem, "Whenever I Went," is a recollection of hunting pheasants with a friend's uncle. Moore fetched the ammo, but was never allowed to plunk the birds. Yes, the hardboiled boozing, the macho-act of hunting, and a colloquial idiom are all here - but the play of line-breaks and enjambments is subtle, almost esoteric, even feminine. Here is how the poem ends:

i
liked to watch him
shoot he almost
never missed limp
pheasants dive
bombing the brush
looked like burnt
pieces of the sun
falling off after
a kill he'd take

a little pull on a
half pint of beam
say it's for the
eyes kid it's for
the eyes

Humor, nausea, topicality, and disgust are hallmarks of *Planet Detroit.* The squeamish need not apply. Nimmo's efforts, like PATRICK MC KINNON's *Poetry Motel,* MERRITT CLIFTON's *Samisdat,* and BELINDA SUBRAMAN's *Gypsy* satisfy poets who seek alternatives to the sleek academic work sponsored by writing programs and the moribund *The American Poetry Review, Poetry Magazine, The Iowa Review*, etc. Taking a cue from HENRY THOREAU's *Life Without Principle,* (a quote occupies the back cover), Nimmo and authors believe that to subvert establishment values is to live one's creative life with principle.

Such a poetry of complaint, protest, and satire, designed to shock the smug power classes has, of course, an ancient history. Since medieval times, broadsides and ballads have been powerful instruments for effecting social change. Old CHAUCER's scatalogical poems reflect a tradition of gross tales--fabliaux offensive to chaste ears, anchored in primal sexual earthiness, and meant for the pubs and the streets.

Populist poetry of yet another sort has an ancient history - sentimental verse celebrating love, children, domestic issues, and facile religious values. The mode is still very much with us, appearing in our magazines, greeting cards, and newspapers. Popular personalities, viz., RAY BRADBURY, LEONARD NIMOY, SUSANNE SHUTZ, and RICHARD THOMAS, among others, write the stuff. Aficionados of such verse, prizing sanitized and sentimental language, cliche of sentiment and social values, would be shocked by *Planet Detroit.*

The latter echoes spirits from the great underground

counter-culture of the 'sixties, inspired and shaped by GINSBERG, BOB DYLAN, ED SANDERS, D. A. LEVY, and JOAN BAEZ. Most *Poetry Detroit* readers constitute an audience of like minds - the Yuppies, the right-wing politicians, the smug and academic poets and critics will go on blithely, untouched by the scathing ironies and sardonic humor found here.

CHARLES BUKOWSKI is, of course, the mentor for many of these writers. Still largely ignored by academic circles, Buk is probably the best-selling serious poet in America. Somebody out there buys and reads him. And according to reports, he is the most famous American poet in Europe. Perhaps it augurs well that the hordes who read Bukowski, and who probably care little about the formalist work of such poets as ROBERT PINSKY, DAVE SMITH, CHARLES WRIGHT, JORIE GRAHAM, BRENDA HILLMAN, WILLIAM MATTHEWS, et al, will occasionally take up *Planet Detroit* or some similar mag, and ream their souls (and colons) with these roto-rooters, lubed with spermacetti angers and fulminations as they are.

Bukowski's *Relentless as the Tarantula* contains a baker's dozen of poems. Some are finger-exercises, some are better than that. The title poem is one of the latter: here, Bukowski assesses personal threat - you can't even sit quietly at a cafe in Europe without being machine-gunned; the presence of humans anywhere on the planet guarantees there'll never be any peace. And right now, something sinister is "working toward you." Some poems are about writing as the sanity-maintaining activity of Bukowski's life. To those fans who think he's a contented man, forget it! "Agony sometimes changes / form / but / it never ceases for / anybody." His incredible fame, he insists, has not turned his head. Relaxation is not in the cards: he sits there typing his ass "straight on through/ it" as he always has done. For the thousandth time he chops at pretentious poets:

all these words - we type away - on and on - most
of us living

lives
quite ordinary and uncourageous - we are sick to
think that
our own
potentials are
exceptional.

I don't like us and I never did - is there anything
more
disgusting
than a writer who tends to write mostly
poetry?

STEVE RICHMOND, son of Bukowski, methadone, and Japanese music, who lives in Los Angeles, a bird-flop or two over from Bukowski, and who is some twenty years younger, presents 19 Gagaku, a title he has used for nearly all of his free-verse, personal litany poems. Gagaku is shinto music which Richmond plays on a record player, as he writes his poems. Demons interweave with moments of peace, viz.,

the demons teeth I suddenly see
have little openings at the bottom of each fang
and multicolored liquid
drips

and, later, this:

it's peaceful here
nobody is bitching at me
I'm content writing poetry

Sadist doctors, the waiting wives of men in prison, women junkies, despisers and railers at Richmond drift through these litanies. The worst days are those when there is no "methadone gulp" and no mail. "People like me, they say," Richmond writes, "have built a bottle around them and now we're stuck inside - but I've a typewriter inside here and my poems (extensions of myself) I can blast out the open bottle mouth - see me?

I'm a cow inside the bottle writing poetry – my cow dream . . . my cow eye dream gone . . . ."

Richmond is a poet who has published since the sixties in obscure places. He is unique, and some enterprising publisher should bring out a Selected Poems. There'll be sifting and winnowing to do, but the result should be stunning. In the meantime, thanks to *Planet Detroit Magazine* for reminding us that Richmond is still around, and writing. And thanks to *Planet Detroit* itself for being here.

POETRY

Vol. 147: No. 5 (February 1986). Editor: Joseph Parisi. Assistant Editor: Jim Elledge. 601 S. Morgan St, Box 4348, Chicago IL 60680. Monthly. $22 per year. 63pp.

In my first *Black and Blue Guide*(1983) I scrutinized an issue of *Poetry* and found it greatly deficient. I return to this dowager periodical now, the MARGARET DUMONT of poetry journals, to see if it deserves still more noisome bunny awards. In the interval, the editors have changed, a fact that excites curiosity, since one hopes that its earlier myopic stress on conservative and academic poets and reviewers is corrected. *Poetry* has seemed a house-organ for a handful of trade and selected university poetry publishers. Small or alternative presses are almost entirely ignored, and most of the poets are prize-winners, poets in demand on the reading circuits, poets with conservative academic degrees, and reviewers who are poets appearing in these hoary pages. I lamented that the daring of the first numbers, edited by HARRIET MONRO and featuring POUND and WILLIAMS long since disappeared among the mushrooms and daffodils of meadows having little or nothing to do with vigorous poetry.

Since this new issue features a passel of ambitious, currently fashionable poets, roughly in their mid-thirties and early forties, things do not augur well. I shall examine these poets in turn.

DAVE SMITH

Smith's poems, to adapt one of his own lines, curl "in sleep like puppies." Sure, he likes surprises, especially when memories of his adolescent sexual awakenings, early boyhood, and the lineaments of his manhood sneak up and goose him. In one such recollection, a nubile sweetie (they are both 19) in a "skin-tight and moon-sluiced" swim suit, "barely pregnant" (aren't you either pregnant or not?), is a turn on. As the waters go "webby with cradled starlight," and "dawn" *lays* "the bar bare" the happy couple treks to the water. As he dawdles, bends "for the blue/of a clam's dome," a schoolboy's image of a vagina, she evanesceses, excusing Smith from having to evoke more sexual odor than might offend a staid reader. He's left, as we are, feeling that the world (and his poem) is "empty."

In "Driving Lesson," Smith teaches a son to drive, and recalls a harrowing experience with his own father. Poems like this are BALL TWISTERS, ie., poems parodying a poet's male *effectualities,* poems that evoke boys twisting their scrotums so that the gonads tighten, ostensibly enlarging their penises. Smith writes many of these.

As for "Driving Lesson," any father who has sought to teach a sibling (I remember the lurch that broke the axle of my dad's Model A) will love this poem - on a first reading. What cheapens Smith are two of his devices: one, he brags about the beauty of his son: he's taller than Smith, scans the horizon "hawk-like," and looks as good as any of those boys on "the videos." And then, once again Smith evokes the trivial recollection so typical of his verse, and writes a tacky imitation of GERARD MANLEY HOPKINS (cf. sonnet, "I wake and feel the fell of dark"): Smith recalls

> **the heap I heaved in my first time, all**
> **the infinite star-dark opened, crying come!**
> **Therefore I will not scream at him.**

This is terrible writing.

In "Championship Fight" Smith's dad drives around in the "big Plymouth," filled with mad energy, jamming the foot-pedal to the floor. The triggering experience is one of his dad's bar fights. The moment, as described, is a pretty decent imitation of HEMINGWAY's prose style:

Yet I saw the black fighter make the spit
lick from that broken mouth before the bar
emptied its first row of booths. It was fast.

Then come the cheap shots (fisticuff poem-feints): the fight somehow harrows the family - mother is left glaring "back at the moon cool on the windshield." Dad calls her "his knockout." Boy-Smith himself remembers curling up in the back seat all dismal and scared, eliciting this commonplace on the brevity of life:

I thought it would be him
crying, peeing blood into a stranger's ditch,
who said Jesus, oh Jesus, it's over so quick.

MOLLY PEACOCK

Not a single one of Peacock's poems required writing: all seem staged, like workshop assignments. There's the pregnancy poem: "The Choice," a timely rendition of a virulent social issue. The spavined, plodding writing sounds faked. Try this passage:

It's not a dead little thing
without a spinal chord yet, but a spirit of
the parent we all ought to have had, of
possibility.

Peacock scribbles her way towards energy which, alas, eludes her. Her poems sink like the proverbial stone, or, if you prefer, float like the soggy doughnut, before she can grab it. I string these lines together to emphasize their inferior quality, even as prose:

> **. . . these choices, not shriveling//but**
> **choice alive with choice, alive with what's**
> **not/taken, or taken up, both pulsing with direc-**
> **tion,/for some mistakes are re-takes, or correc-**
> **tion,/past times that were forasken now held when**
> **caught.**

The closing lines play woefully on moors and harbors:

> **The thought of the pregnancy somehow unmoors**
> **the anxiety the choice still harbors.**

"Prayer," a bit better, presents an intriguing character Herbie who tells the world how important it is to pray on dates, and to show affection sitting in church, "Neath the weight of our bowed heads in stained light." The poem is an acrostic, spelling HOLDING HANDS IN CHURCH NOW down the right side, a cute device, which here doesn't add up to much. Conclusion: "When we hold hands now it is as necessary: /flesh is still the church."

STEPHEN DOBYNS

Dobyns is the writer that Peacock and Smith will never be. Despite some false steps, his imagination is usually on target, his voice deft, original, and sure, and he has a variety of themes and topics. "The Invitation" is a fable of one of those lives in which "nothing goes right." They fail even at suicide: the pills won't stay down, the arm gets caught in the noose, they miss "the last train," one they'd hoped to throw themselves beneath. In Heaven, they're the same screw-ups they were on earth:

> **If a loser**
> **like that can enter heaven, then how is it**
> **an honor for us to be here as well -**
> **those of us who are totally deserving?**

Our hero, from his "little cloud house," watches the sun set over planet Earth, commiserates with all the folk there bustling about, and weeps - though secretly, since "in heaven crying is forbidden." Some of those tears fall to earth, striking a salesman who is "rushing/between Point A and Point B."

> **The salesman slips**
> **staggers and stops as if slapped in the face.**
> **People on the street think he's crazy or drunk.**
> **Why am I selling ten thousand ballpoint pens?**
> **he asks himself. Suddenly his only wish is to**
> **dance the tango.**

"Cemetery Nights V" turns on the original motif of some dead folk, already crumbling, emerging from graves facing those more recently dead who linger outside the Eternity-fence waiting to get in:

> **So arranged the dead form a great spoked wheel -**
> **such is the firey wheel that rolls through heaven.**

Throw in a few rats, a scarecrow/dead husband gazing down into his house where his wife sits in his favorite chair, drinks his wine, and copulates with a lover in his bed and you have most of the remaining furniture of this easily forgettable poem.

"Theseus Within the Labyrinth" is an improvisation on a classical motif made entirely relevant to contemporary life.

The tone is casual, even whimsical:

> **As for the Minotaur, lounging**
> **on his couch, nibbling grapes and sipping wine, while**
> **a troop of ex-virgins fluttered to his beck and call,**
> **Theseus must have scared the horns right off him,**

slamming back the door and standing there in his lion
skin suit and waving that ugly club.

The moral is Aesopian:

Better to be ignorant, to go into the future as into
a long tunnel, without ball of yarn or clear direction,
to tiptoe forward like any fool or saint or hero,
jumpy, full of second thoughts and bravely unprepared.

"Querencia," some 150 lines long, explores the situation of a doomed bull in a ring: "it is the bull's business to be dragged away." Potentially the best of Dobyns' poems, this one is a failure. He's much too loquacious, drawing out parallels between the bull's condition and ours. The homelitic passages go on and on. Among various meanings, "querencia" refers to that place a man or animal chooses, a place most cared about, where he feels secure and protected:

In the ring, it may be a spot near the gate
or the place he was first hurt or where
the sand is wet or where there's a little blood,
his querencia, even though it looks like any
other part of the ring, except this is the spot
the bull picks as his home, the place he will
defend and keep returning to . . . .

The moral is too drawn out, tedious. We all hope for the clean kill, and aren't always lucky. Dobyns recalls a boyhood visit to Barcelona where he saw a youthful matador miss his kill: the bull had to be stabbed by an assistant, who severed the spinal chord, leaving the matador disgraced. Dobyns needs to know that less is often more. Flashing the message requires nearly a hundred lines, none of them possessing distinction.

OTHERS

RALPH BURNS zaps us with "Debris", again in the casual style typical of this gaggle of *Poetry* poets. He's at the table "writing." The garbage truck goes by (and we're treated to what's in the cans). He considers his reflection in a mirror, wondering why he can't look himself straight in the eye. Then, it comes! He's been carrying guilt around for not telling his dad, who phones to say he loves the son, that he in turn loves the father:

When he called and spoke his love
I only listened and laughed

a shrugging, invulnerable laugh . . . .

Dad shortly shoots himself, leaving behind a guilt-ridden, grieving son.

Dad
kills himself thoroughly, again and again,
. . . puts the .410 to his chin
and its drizzling outside and the phone rings
and we're sleeping.

STEPHEN COREY writes a vaporous, genteel thing on dreams and sentimentality. The dullest lines are the final four:

I reach the sun-drenched edge and I know
I have cut off the dullness of reason
to set loose a burgeoning dream
that could give all my other dreams range.

Like MOLLY PEACOCK, STEPHEN DUNN seems to write without any urgency. "All That We Have" is a tedious play on easy abstractions, dully phrased ("happily or otherwise" - mostly "otherwise") which ends with this schlock:

The man coming in now
to the woman.
The woman going out to the man.

"Sleeping With Ghosts" is also uninspired. What do you think about when you go to a guest house and sleep overnight in an antique bed where numerous other no-longer-living folk slept? Well, you think of their ghosts, some wronged in their lives, others assuring you that life is good, etcetera. Eventually, you join them, "without fear, in a world wholly theirs." "Aerial in the Pines" chops off the top of a "majestic pine" to afford a less impeded view of the landscape: "The tree looked foolish, like someone/well-dressed/with a bad haircut . . . ."

ALLISON FUNK gives us the ghost of ELINOR WYLIE "jealous" of EDNA ST. VINCENT MILLAY. I guess this transpires at the MacDowell Colony where the legend persists. The best moment is a description of wood ferns as "as delicate as underclothing."

"Forms of Conversion" is a trendy, brainy poem about COPERNICUS, trade, fishing, blood types, parents, and rabbis. "Elegy" is about the ease of birthing in the desert near Jerusalem. "The desert is more honest," Funk says, without giving us the other half of the comparison. Easy. Easy.

DAVID CLEWELL writes a six-page take on astral travel. I can't find a thing to recommend anyone's reading it. It's slack, cute, and facile. Here's a sample of one of the numerous coy, fey moments. He's leaving his body for the astral plane:

When I stepped off into thin air
and looked down at myself in bed,
I could clearly see I'd gone too far.

Here the solipsistic self released into the "Great Beyond" draws on tacky old W. C. FIELDS films:

What I got was the Obligatory Beyond:
people I'd somehow managed to outlive
on parade through a long home movie of the dead.

Then follows a procession of family members, teachers, and fellow WW II soldiers. There's not a single flash of insight or originality along the tedious route. Here's the final wisdom:

Because when we come back, it's always
right where we left off: the middle
of a night, a room where the phone never rings
or it never stops ringing.

BARRY GOLDENSOHN's impressive "The Toy" recounts the failures of a man who remained more of a wind-up toy than a man, and the issue of comedy: Says ARISTOTLE: "the comic figures we love/are smaller than life and shrink/as we laugh and loom above." Though we diminish this little man with our laughter, so that he falls between "tight floorboards," we hear what sounds like Chaplinesque pain (my idea): "the intimate howl of his gears." Don't feel contempt for others who provoke risiblity in us, they may be far more profound than we know.

MARIE HOWE's "Lullaby" recounts the failure of her mother's efforts to guard the daughter from a harsh life - the poem is honest, crisply detailed, moving - as is her "Apology." This moment half-way through shows her writing at its best:

Even now, as you desire me, my mother is
stirring the question
into the burning soup as my father's mouth closes,
the one hundred and nine years between them

walking away
like a man who has knocked on the wrong door.

THE REVIEWS

VERNON SHETLEY, who signs in with a PhD from Columbia and who teaches at Wellesley, writes tediously and academically about seven (count 'em) poetry books, all either from trade presses or from university presses: Atheneum is represented twice; Knopf, Houghton Mifflin, William Morrow, Ecco (one of the DANIEL HALPERIN enterprises), and Ithaca House (Cornell University). What continues to amaze me about *Poetry*'s fondness for these houses is that, from all reports, they treat their poets far more dismally than good alternative presses do, rarely keep books in print for more than a season after they appear, must be struggled with before any meaningful promotion occurs, and wind off selling fewer copies than, again, our best small presses do. Numerous poets have complained to me about these matters - and I can name names. Why can't a lit mag as influential as *Poetry* (or, at least, as well-read - I assume it's read, although most of its subscriptions, I understand, go to public libraries) wake up and begin to serve those exciting poets out there who aren't on the short short lists of the trade houses?

Since, I assume, *Poetry* enjoys its arts foundations grants, and other public funding, shouldn't that funding be cut off until the editor demonstrates his willingness to serve a much larger community than he now does?

One case in point: Why waste more pages on reviewing the already much-reviewed Atheneum poets? The editors of Atheneum have informed me that they have a "closed list," and will keep publishing a stable of aging, largely mediocre poets. And so it goes. Dear poet, expect not to find your books reviewed in *Poetry* unless you can boast similar publishing credentials. And don't waste postage sending poems here unless you similarly qualify. If you are a relatively unpublished poet, have a good University Writing Program address, or have a first book about to appear from one of the approved publishers, proceed. Most poets in this issue have reputations.

The best poet for my money, CHRISTOPHER BUCKLEY (Ithaca House), is the only one receiving a severe wrist-slap. Shetley's commentaries on the other figures are vapid, yeah, even toadying.

DENNIS SCHMITZ writes so "slow" that his "brief poems have time to work." A typical poem by DS "would make a scant paragraph in prose, yet for the most part, he avoids the techniques of compression that traditionally allow poets to say much in small compass." He likes the "deadpan treatment." Sounds to me as if Schmitz is dull; Shetley, though, fakes compliments.

CARL DENNIS receives praise for arriving "almost at a zero degree of understatment." Can you go lower than that? One has to admire Dennis's "patient reticence," Shelty avers, his "refusal to force" himself "upon our attention." Again, if you read between the lines, Dennis is boring - never trust Shetley to be honest enough to say so though.

DAVID ST. JOHN is admirable because his poems "have the breathless, impersonal urgency of a telegram." "Shadowy personages" whose minds are "far too fine to be violated by ideas" drift through. What an excuse for mental vacuity! To Shetley's credit, he does protest that St. John doesn't always handle the telegram style well. His poems "fall apart into separate lyric movements."

As for JOHN UPDIKE, Shetley strains to place him within a tradition of earlier novelists who also wrote poems: SCOTT, HARDY, and MELVILLE. The time Shetley wastes setting up his argument implies that he knows Updike is no damn good, and he lacks the courage to face up. Once he does proceed, his take on Updike is a marvel of toadyism. While Updike "is not naturally a poet," his poems have come to "demand" judging by serious poetic standards. Take heart Updike. Shetley will always treat you as the great writer you are, although your poetry falls short. Here Shetley wants to tread on your velvet slippers, but falls back short of the toes: "Updike does on occasion rouse his powers of verbal exuberance, but at times the results are hard to welcome."

HOWARD MOSS deserves praise because he realizes his great limitations, his "minor-key plangency," and goes on developing and refining his art within those limitations. Moss has abandoned some of his "highly self-conscious early" manner for "a progressive movement toward rhetorical openness and metrical relaxation" (I read this as "dullness"). Moss's "performance is never less than perfectly artful." And so on, and so on. I guess that to disguise complaints as compliments is what one would expect of almost any reviewer tackling Moss, one of the top czars of current poetry - he is, after all, poetry editor of *The New Yorker*, as every poet - and reviewer - knows.

Shetley is less gingerly with JAMES MERRILL who has never managed to devise "a truly public idiom for public subjects: the fault, I suspect, is in the moment and not the man." Yet, there's more flattery here than complaint, and, of course, Merrill is one of our institutions, though he edits no magazine.

Now, the very things Shetley praises in the other poets, the illusion "of having no style at all," he disavows in CHRISTOPHER BUCKLEY. One of the put-downs is that Buckley is "a sort of EDWARD HOPPER of verse, sedimenting the poignance of the quotidian in flat, drab surfaces." Nice sounding academic observation that. I've re-read Buckley's *Other Lives* and find many exciting passages, fresh, complex, and imaginative. Is there something of a bully in Shetley the critic? Sure, he's not always cowardly, though he takes on the easy meat, boys. Buckley is the less-known, though not the less-seasoned, of this lot of poets.

IN CONCLUSION, I see no evidence whatsoever of any improvement in *Poetry* over my earlier critique of 4 years ago. The poets write just as badly, as pretentiously, as safely. All of them either teach at the better-known writing programs or universities, or they edit magazines that perpetuate the dismal sort of writing featured here: they edit *Crazyhorse* and *The Georgia Review,* and teach at Tufts, Dartmouth, Skidmore, Wellesley, Warren Wilson College, Webster University, Brandeis, Endicott,and Columbia. *Poetry* pays almost no attention to alternative presses. I repeat what I said earlier: all public support monies should be withdrawn from *Poetry* until they do more to serve a broad spectrum of American poets. The best poets, DOBYNS and HOWE, can't bring this tedious issue into balance.

POETRY AUSTRALIA

Number 100 (1985). Editor: Grace Perry. Assoc. and Contributing Editors: Ronald Dunlop, Bruce Beaver, Philip Benham, James Tulip. Managing Editor: John Millett. South Head Press (The Market Place, Berrima New South Wales 2577, Australia). $25 Per year.

For longevity, *Poetry Australia* must rank among the the hoariest of all literary magazines. This issue, the one hundredeth, commemorates twenty-one years of vigorous publishing, and is a characteristic mix of American and Commonwealth poets with Australasian poets. Featured are lengthy poems by LOUIS SIMPSON, KEITH RUSSELL, NORMAN TALBOT, and a generous sampling of my own *Hawthorne*.

In a commemorative essay, PETER MURPHY seeks "threads of consciousness" in Australian poets. What he finds is a fascination with the vastness and the diversity of the land, a mix of "suppressed guilt" and joy over a land untimely ripped from the native aborigines; an insecurity over the brevity of human life; and the use of the vastness of sky and landscape as conduits for the transcendental experience - "the merging of the microcosm and the macrocosm - in which our own features are discovered in the world outside and the world outside is perceived within us . . . "

This impressive journal, and the Australian poets it features, is the direct result of the incredible energy, taste, and supportive zest of one of the rarest, most unsung patron-poets at work today - GRACE PERRY. She has discovered and encouraged a host of poets who might not otherwise be published - one of her stars is JOHN MILLET, a poet I have come greatly to admire. His *Tail-Arse Charlie*, poems on a WW II War Ace, has been widely reviewed in the United States. Grace Perry has had many active lives, as a doctor of medicine with a huge practice, as a rancher, and as a shaper of culture.

We need her autobiography.

Nearly all poets here write free verse, though most employ traditional cadences. There are a scattering of sonnets but without end-rhymes. Language is usually traditional. A moment like this one from BARRY O'DONOHUE's "Nam" is rare:

A bond between countries is a black hole
they are falling into; America, Australia
are sharing the Pacific, are fucking
beneath Hawaii.

O'Donohue's "Nam" is a complex evocation of the Viet Nam experience, one of the best on the theme.

These poets often love ornate language. PETER KIRKPATRICK's description of an octopus on a fisherman's line is energetic:

. . . it was an exotic orange bloom on his line
that throbbed shut, to a red bud, squirting
like a joke buttonhole.

Here, KEITH RUSSELL describes a view from a train crossing a flooded landscape. He blends both interior and exterior views:

The train south inches its way
across the flooded part
water lillies adrift snagged by twigs
all the passengers lean to windows
open doors and stare as the train
moves like a string of barges
wheels in water

The passage is particularly apt, since Russell is taking a long journey home after seeing his father through his final illness and death. "A Sugar Bag Filled with Fish" is a first-rate poem on a much-written about, often sentimentally treated, theme. Russell's lines are as lean as short weather-warped boards:

> **I saw**
> **his spirit break**
> **seven years before**
> **this turn like a horse snap**
> **and snap the rope**
> **clean much cleaner than**
> **the surgeon's art he broke his life**
> **by giving up the dead**
> **a history overboard**
> **a sugar bag full of fish**
> **droped like an anchor**
> **without chain no way to**
> **bring it back no way held**
> **now his life drifted**
> **seven years this way and that . . . .**

Here are more quotes from this amazing poem, Parts Four and Five, concluding the poem. Normally, I would not quote so extensively since the truly curious reader could write to get most magazines under review - but though *Poetry Australia* is far away, I urge readers to order copies and subscribe. Russell is on a train:

> FOUR
>
> **Some near death manage to**
> **shake off the debris become lucid**
> **without reference without object**
> **speak a kind of logic never to**
> **be toppled they lock in like**
> **a football star see the ball**
> **see the line and they're over**
> **But no action is performed**
> **the world as mantle falls**
> **slipped through escaped. . ."**

FIVE

All the effort to overcome
the tins buckets tubs tanks reservoirs
of water water water

Beside me sits a woman mad part
of the second world war
gives me wine and offers
straight off to buy my testicles
Near Taree she suggests she might
"Cut out ya nuts go better on a
woman I could love me a woman
strong woman love me and make
woman babies"

I eat for breakfast
the last of the funeral cake
leave the train
walk home and sleep
wake in dream
and see my father is dead
and buried

PETER LLOYD fashions moving studies of a dying old man in a park feeding black swans (death figures) and of an ancient librarian tottering among the shelves in a computerized age. Here are a few lines from "The black swans":

Apricot mornings like this among the trees
in the park,
send the old man mad with desire –
but his cough drives them apart
coming up into his throat warm & soft as
phlegm;
his stick taps while a small breeze,
stretched tight,
scatters the dahlia heads which sway like
red
penicillin lampshades lit from underneath,

frail as human
skin . . . .

MARK O'CONNOR returns to his home town after a decade or so, evokes both painful and delicious memories, and laments bulldozers, council housing estates, and the neatness that has tamed and destroyed the town:

I see in today's neat roses, the roofed
crate
where the Christmas goose was penned
hissing and fattening, and the amazing deep
hole
where Dad buried the neck and gizzards
too deep for the dog, until six months later
I found and re-hid them in a sacred spot.

To this boy "a crayfish in the town drain is proof of the Amazon," a blackbird is "all ornithology," and the mouse in the henyard "is wild as a dragon / and takes his father three nights to kill." To all this, of course, the city planners are immune.

The featured poet is LOUIS SIMPSON, with a thirteen page, single poem, "The Previous Tenant." The whole, a complex personal history, written in Simpson's most deceptively simple style, appears in his *The Best Hour Of The Night* (Ticknor & Fields/Houghton Mifflin, 1983).

I have read a baker's dozen numbers of *Poetry Australia* and find all of them as impressive as # 100. The editors encourage exchanges with American poets, and are enthusiastic about contributions - do though include postal coupons if you wish your manuscripts returned. They pay in contributors copies and a free subscription to the journal.

POETRY/LA

(#10, Spring/Summer 1985). Editor: Helen Friedland. Box 84271, Los Angeles CA 90073. 124 pp. Semiannual. $8 per year.

Of the 55 poets here, four are Hungarian (translated by Los Angeles poet and citizen of the world JASCHA KESSLER), one is from Texas and another is from Minnesota. The rest hail from Los Angeles and environs. I applaud the focus - what other metropolis has so fat a journal devoted to its writers? and to young writers?

Yet, when I examine *Poetry/LA* I am dismayed. Of 100 poems only 19 (count 'em) are worth reading a second time, 37 are so awful one is amazed to find them published anywhere, and 44 are mediocre. This journal contains some of the worst poetry being written in LA.

The editor's bias is obviously for the First Person, or Ego poem. Sixty poems are as lavish with *I*s and *us*es as oat kernels in a hen's craw. One of the worst, "Slow Nightmares," by MIMA PEREIRA has these: "I don't know," "I need to tell you," "I have lots of time," and "I won't / allow you more / than a corner / of my / tight dreams." JACK GRAPES's "White Wall" is studded with these phrases: "I come," "I leave," I mean," I know," "I am staring at." When he winds off with a metaphysical interrogation: "What time is it? / What time is it, really?" we don't much care.

The editor is also fond, it appears, of what I call Baby Talk Poems. NELS CHRISTIANSON writes pat-a-cake verses, apparently intended for amusing a child: "I have a boy / I have a boy named / I have a boy in my skin . . . " RACHELLE BEVENISTE, seeing herself as a "lost" child, writes: "Down down until I see / a child sitting at a table / her hands in her lap." RICARDO ANGELO improvises baby-talk: "She be fresh / my love / she kisses me. // She be fresh / lying in the grass. // She be fresh / a light summer rain . . . ." MICHAEL BERNSTEIN sees in berries on a rowan tree "baby fist fists / ruthless / encircling the nipple / the sap does this / pulls itself / against the suck of / gravity on its own terms . . . ."

One of the very worst passages appears in GERALD LOCKLIN's "Self-Portraits": "what need do we have / with two ears, / two nostrils, / two penises? // after all, you can only pee / through one nostril at a time." BETSEY WARWICK, RALPH S. CARLSON, and STEVE ROOD are close seconds. Warwick: "I feel the / closeness / of you / the knot / of your / hard body." Carlson writes yet another of those weak turn-on poems:

Our clockless world
sweats pleasure a-dream in candlelight.
Moist and naked,
we drift away from all we own.
You stroke my cheek.
I cup my hand to your breast.
. . . .
I cup your breast.
You stroke my thigh.

STEVE ROOD measures his life, "to its long / clarity," and takes "you" (I guess it's his sweetie) "slowly / allowing you to spread / like a natural pool." SUSANNE SHUTZ, RAY BRADBURY, and LEONARD NIMOY where are you when we need you?

CAROL LEM has mastered many bad workshop mannerisms of diction and attitude: she waits "in the slow dark" for "bones of silence." She needs "adagios / wine / a light rain." MICHAEL BERNSTEIN writes of "an act of passion" and "the slow will," but can't get off without some very spavined echoes of W. B. YEATS: "Where thaw becomes / the furl / of dogwood I have come / inviolate and / silent to this wood / the yew the beech . . . ." Awards for the worst poems go to DONNA HILBERT's "Ode to Old Men at Breakfast" and SHIRLEY WINWARD's "Letters from the Aegean."

Hilbert counts the "liver spots" on male seniors in a cafe. Winward trips to the Aegean, where she swims "on sapphire waves" and kisses "the hills of Thessaly."

Most poets are preoccupied with mundane matters. Open *Poetry/LA* almost anywhere and you find openings like these: "It has been a good / day," "Will I wake up? or remain torpid," "I go north, up to the mountains," "as morning begins."

Still, 19 poems invite some rejoicing. These are by CHARLES BUKOWSKI, ELOISE KLEIN HEALY, ROBERT HARRIS, NICHOLA MANNING, and KENNETH LINCOLN (the best of them all).

Old pro BUKOWSKI supplies the usual 90 proof poems we expect of him, set in his venues - a tacky LA bar and a steamy apartment in the early morning. He's been up all night writing, listening to freeway noise, drinking, watching cable TV. His cats follow him upstairs:

fine fellows, we have no discontent, we have
no
arguments, we listen to the same music,
never vote for
a president.
one of the cats, the big one, leaps on the
back
of my chair, rubs against my shoulders and
neck.

Bukowski won't read poems to the felines. One cat "leaps to the floor and walks out to the / balcony and his buddy / follows. // they sit and watch the night; we have the / power of sanity here."

"My Vanishing Act" is Bukoswki at his best. There's no surplusage, and he is underplayed, self-ironic, and winsome. When he gets sick of being in the bar he goes off to a field near an "abandoned" graveyard:

I didn't consider this to be a
moribund pastime,
it just seemed to be the
place to be.

He meditates on the headstones, seen through the grasses, through his "vicious hangover." If he falls asleep there, nobody will bother him. When he returns to the bar, the patrons will say they thought he'd died:

I was their bar freak, they needed me
to make themselves feel
better . . . .

Each of ELOISE KLEIN HEALEY's trio is keenly felt and well-crafted. She is that special poet who writes the "I" poem with grace. In her elegy for ROBERT DEUTSCH, the Northridge poet and teacher, her closing stanza is inventive, compassionate, tender, and wise in its parallels between poems/writing and death and love:

Everything of paper, so easy
to unpeel the stars and fold their points
back into darkness.
Unwrap the man
down to the skeleton of wire
and from the heart
unfold the folded fortune
to its promised length.
Even that is paper,
but we put on it a life.

Once you've gotten past ROBERT HARRIS' complicated (possibly pretentious) title, "A Landscape By Caspar David Friedrich As Spied Through Gabriele D'Annunzio's Garden Window by Luchino Visconti," you find a marvellous poem. Harris captures much of Visconti's deft decadence, the Italionate hot-house, supra-civilized beauty lavish with baroque death leering nearby. Here is a sampling:

My day blends a bit
fine it blends the colors
into spectral stains of venetian glass
giving the eyes a texture
of pointillistic jabs way out of period
. . . .
Pristine grounds allow for no shadows
allow for no accidents as gowns tugged
by overgrowth, no tumbling to Schumann
no reawakening in arms glossed with rivulets
tracing, slicking

Niccolo, cracks in the bullet hacked Mars
can be picked up on camera despite the thin
whitewash
of our decade listen to those crickets in
this steam
wheel me out past the empty urns
the long way

NICHOLA MANNING writes on paintings by SEURAT and KANDINSKY.

Here she evokes Seurat's style:

Even the water is made of dots and holes
but the oarsmen thrust through like a load
and everyone wears hats like bowling balls;
have bodies shaped like bombs that may
explode.

Kandinsky inspires memorable Surrealist writing that hints of holocausts:

This is the fire of strings and eyelashes
and icecream melting on the blue-green
flames.

To put it out they try steel wire splashes
till only the edge of one mountain remains.
Somebody is lighting a cigarette.

KENNETH LINCOLN's 5 poems were written in Florence, Italy where he went to research "contemporary Euro-American images of the American Indian." He chairs the graduate program in American Indian Studies at UCLA. Florentine light evokes memories of a Nebraska boyhood: "Oats, barley, sorghum, rye, flax . . . ./ A kerosene / Lantern yellow against the prairie snow . . . ." In Florence, an "unfiltered and seasonal" light returns:

The yellows gather like a host of exiled
Saffron angels whispering their shades
Of sandstone resurrection . . . .

My favorite poem is "Florentine Citizen," a keenly-felt evocation of Michelangelo sculpting. Here is the entire poem:

FLORENTINE CITIZEN
That sculptor with the smashed nose is up
To it again! Out in the garden with ruined
Stone late at night, a candle in his cap -
Why doesn't he write something instead?
Sonnets, or terza rima, any damn
Thing but this tchink, tchink, tchink.
You'd think he slept with marble, not just
His workers, as the nuns suspect. I'll bet
He never finishes half those statues.
And what's it now, another Pieta,
One more mother with a dead son?
Some fine young life-size boy to stroke
With chisels? What's this, fist, chest,
Drilled eyes, David after the kill?

I can only hope that my severity will stimulate the editor to cultivate more discretion in selecting future work. Wouldn't it be better to have a *Poetry/LA* of 50 quality pages rather than one padded with embarrassing work? Los Angeles deserves better. Some of the better-known poets (LOCKLIN, KOERTGE, ATCHITY, and MC CLOSKEY) submitted inferior work.

Any literary magazine with so specialized a locale--Milwaukee, Toledo, Boise, Kansas City, Anaheim--risks packing itself with fiber not worth chewing; there may just not be enough talent around to justify an issue. Yet, generating pride in a literary community is desirable. The question persists: does *Poetry/LA* provide a truly nourishing image of such a community? As the journal reaches the wider world, will it be ignored, jeered, and held up as evidence that Los Angeles is one of the foul tar-pits of contemporary verse? I fear so.

Another issue is that young poets are published before they develop a voice. HELEN FRIEDLANDER, the editor, in a preface, discusses this complaint. She takes on ROBERT BLY who in "Early Publishing" (*Coda*, June 1981), argues that the young poet by seeing work in print will almost never improve. Friedlander disagrees. I think that Bly is right and Friedlander is wrong. The rare rare poet (where is our KEATS, our SHELLEY?) will certainly develop whether he's published or not. However, most poet-siblings, still drooling mashed peas and liver, will feel indeed professional, and will continue the slobberings that got them into print in the first place. I've taught writing workshops too long to know that they'll do otherwise. And when a journal sponsors publishing parties at which many of these poets read their writing, the problem of ego and undeserved and unearned self-gratulation worsens. Perhaps one solution is for a journal to publish a quarterly supplement, on newsprint, of work by young poets, much as poems would be xeroxed for consideration in a workshop. The idea would be that these works are not professional, that they are indeed pieces *in progress*. So, encourage the babes, but don't ruin your magazine with their amateurish work. Poetry everywhere, including Los Angeles, needs all the first-rate exposure it can get. *Poetry/LA,* please do better.

THE REAPER

No. 13 (1985). Editors: Robert McDowell & Mark Jarman. 325 Ocean View Ave, Santa Cruz, CA 95062. 3-4 issues per year. 4 issues for $7, institutions $10.

The Reaper, feisty and iconoclastic, floats opinions on the state of contemporary verse, and pleases only itself. Ye olde scythe whips off barley, rye, and buckwheat heads without fear or favor of anyone. All this it does with great panache, with the toughness of a farmer facing a phalanx of conglomerate tractors threatening to put him out of business. A primary tool is satire. There's no other lit mag around so on the mark. All libraries featuring contemporary writing should subscribe and then display the journal where it can be seen and read. The poetry reflects the strong interests of the editors in what they call "narrative" and in well-crafted, often rhymed verse. They are in no sense avant garde (whatever that means.)

THE SATIRE

Here they cut swaths through two currently fashionable, self-serving anthologies, *The Morrow Anthology of Younger American Poets: with an introduction by Anthony Hecht* edited by DAVID SMITH and DAVID BOTTOMS, and *New American Poets of the 80's*, edited by JACK MYERS and ROGER WEINGARTEN (Wampeter Press). I've had my say on these abortions elsewhere (GARGOYLE MAGAZINE), and am delighted to see them assessed here. The more the word is spread, the better.

In *The Reaper*'s FOREVER YOUNG: A SURVEY the editors have solicited responses to the *New* and *Younger* anthologies from readers who have no "immediate stake in the reception of the anthologies." Excluded are chairpeople of English and Writing departments and professional or personal friends of the contributors. Among these "fair Readers" are a clinical psychologist, an attorney, a high school English teacher, a DJ, and the chairman of the Columbus, Ohio Reading Club.

The psychiatrist, Lynn Cannella, Ph.D., of New York City, limits his scrutiny to the outsides of the books, as "signs." Both are "cumbersome oversized paperbacks." One costs $17.95, the other $9.95, for roughly the same poundage. A "high tech" design graces the Morrow book; the Wampeter gray and red are "the power colors of the 1980's" and are seen most often on businessmen and government officials--a gray suit and a red tie. Photographs of all poets appear in the Morrow, none in the Wampeter--which fact "might amount to some psychological mainfestation." Observes Cannella: "Reading of the murderer's crimes, we want to see his picture." If *Younger American Poets* had taken age 40 as the cut-off, ie., birth year of 1945, Smith "would have had to suppress a legitimate desire to be included . . . ." Canella notes: "Had each anthology printed work only by those poets it included under the age of forty, the Morrow book would have been reduced by 37 poets and the Wampeter by 24."

Lawyer Hubert Jeffries, of Tempe, AZ, finds that no editor managed to "devise a compelling argument for this own selection process and the chosen material." Too many poets "leave too much out of their poems." Only 20 are worth re-reading in the Morrow anthology, and a mere 16 in the Wampeter. Here is a devastating comment: "Is it possible that some poets write about subjects that they do not thoroughly understand andcreate characters they do not know and cannot believe in?" Touché!

Ward Justin's Alhambra, CA high schoolers are dismayed to find that "young" is so violated, and are sickened by the fact that Herbert Scott is 54! Nor do they find the introductions helpful. ANTHONY HECHT'S preface to the Morrow put them off because of "gobbledygook." They cite his phrase "a certain prudential canineness," as a case in point. The pictures are a turn-off--most poets appear "sullen." Some students liked DIANE ACKERMAN's photo with airplane, and "expressed a desire to fly her."

Austin Auberge, of KGBO, Detroit, chose favorites, read some, then invited listeners to call in over his Poetry Happy Hole program. AI, FORCHÉ, OLDS, MCHUGH, DENIS JOHNSON, and GARY SOTO got plusses--most of the other poets are bad: of TOM LUX Auberge writes: his "last name sure reflects his poetic good fortune in getting into so many of these shopping cart collections." The Reading Club folk, of Columbus, loathed ANTHONY HECHT's comments on lyric poetry, and busied themselves looking for evidence of "narrative." Only 10% of the poems in the Morrow, and 12% in the Wampeter "are more or less narrative"--enough for a pair of modest chapbooks, no more. Think of all the trees that might have been spared!

THE POETRY

The showcase piece is a portion of a play, by GEORGE KEITHLEY, *The Best Blood of the Country,* based on the life of Aaron Burr. This, the first scene of Act III, is preceded by a short dissertation on the nature of verse drama. Keithley strives, he says, for "a flexible accentual line suitable to speech rhythms which change as the dramatic tension increases or lessens." These speculations, with the model of the play that follows, may be more important than the play itself: perhaps Keithley will stimulate a discussion of the nature of verse drama, as viable today. My own feeling (I have adapted two of my recent books for the stage and am acting in them) is that poetic drama is possible without forcing idioms (even earlier ones) into old dramatic wineskins, which I feel Keithley does.

Burr has just killed Alexander Hamilton, and on an island in the Ohio River is orgainzing a rag-tag army which he intends to use for attacking New Orleans and conquering Mexico. In addition to Burr, there are a chorus (consisting of Burr's recruits), Burr's daughter

Theo, and a freed slave William Love. It may be unfair to judge what appears an ambitious work on the impression made by these few pages. However, I find my mind wandering, and the speeches self-consciously declamatory rather than felt. Perhaps the problem is in Keithley's striving after stale verse music. Here Burr seems more attentive to the mildly Shakespearean turn of language than real emotion. His daughter, appearing as an officer of the regiment, is faintly silly:

BURR.

Let the lads go cross-eyed on claret
or corn liquor. Let them be
whiskey-dizzy, so they slaughter
a sober President who'd rather
bed his black beauty than wage war.
But their drill's done. Dismiss them.

THEO (*steps forward, hands on hips*).

Halt! . . .Fall out!

FREDERICK MORGAN's "Facetiae" is a delicious rhyming romp, in seven parts, through topics literary and juvenile. T.S. Eliot dislikes having to remove his clothes in heaven, a situation rendered with an OGDEN NASH turn:

When Eliot arrived up in heaven
he found it was nothing like church
and suspected that Lancelot Andrewes
had left him somehow in the lurch,
for they forced him to take all his clothes off
and scamper about in the sun--
where he cut a preposterous figure
instead of a dignified one.

Another riff finds EMILY DICKINSON extolling the pleasures of masturbatory "savage joys." There's a pair of poems about a couple of Yeatsian women. In this one, Jane is not quite crazy:

Jane did it today--
will she do it tomorrow?
Not easy to say.
Today she gave way,
but such wary girls may
prefer parting's sweet sorrow
to raptures today.
***Will* she do it tomorrow?**

My favorite poem is by TONY CURTIS, a commemoration of the photographer O. WINSTON LINK, done up as a villanelle. The time: 1956. Link is photographing a smooching couple in the saloon of a train. Here is one stanza:

Link's wired-up lamps, set to jewel the gloom
Flashlight the upholstered Fifties and display
The smooching couple in the chrome saloon.

MAURYA SIMON's poem to a sleeping child, newly born, to whom she is "aunt and stranger," is deft, despite some flirting with platitudes. Here, for example, she inverts a cliché of wisdom: ". . . the weak survive, / and the strong sink into misfortune. / What does it mean to be alive? / Only that we should hunger." And her awarding of a "flexed finger pointing the way" to a road (the Road of Life?) is not calculated to send you rushing for more of her poems. There's an image of the Statue of Liberty, from which the speaker seems exiled; she abstracts a closing benediction recited over the sleeping five-day-old child. I feel let down:

I hear how she [Miss Liberty] calls to each of us,
not just to the homeless, bedraggled
orphans abandoned by wars, poverty.
What she says is what I would say
to you, Joshua, on your fifth worldly day
extend your clenched palms, reach beyond
your body, open your eyes.

CHASE TWITCHELL's "Out of Earshot" is tough

and original: this wise woman knows when to hold back, and let her man, who has not quite matured, be himself. He is only twenty, it appears, and is studying himself in a mirror. He's wearing her gray silk kimono: "cloth from the sea or from heaven, / scattered with white barnacles." He wipes shower steam from some of the mirror, the better to admire himself. She, watching, is tempted to "teach him to be a magnet / to the things he loves." She resists, and in a a superb gesture, allows him his freedom, and her own lovingly expressed wisdom, a special affection:

But he is elsewhere, out of earshot,
and does not yet dwell
on the delicacy of hot water,
or the pleasure of the foot
pressed to a grid of cold tiles.

Like the first hard pears of winter,
he will ripen on a snowy afternoon,
within himself a wedding
of the juice to the slight grit.

I want to read more of Twitchell.

Poets wishing to send work to *The Reaper* might first query, to see what the backlog is like. There aren't all that many poems per issue. And if you succeed in appearing you may polish your poetry medal with special pride: you'll find a discerning, appreciative, and growing readership. *Reaper* folk in conjunction with the Nicholas Roerich Museum, New York, have also started publishing books, as the Story Line Press. VERN RUTSALA's sixth collection, *Backtracking*, is just out. In 1986 they expect to publish books by FREDERICK POLLOCK, TONY CURTIS, and ROBERT McDOWELL.

TEMBLOR

TEMBLOR (#2, 1985). Editor Leland Hickman. 4624 Cahuenga Blvd. #307, N. Hollywood, CA 91602. 136pp. 2 issues for $16.

This expensive, glossy, professionally designed journal features work by CLAYTON ESHLEMAN, JOHN TAGGART, SUSAN HOWE, and CHARLES BERNSTEIN. The editor's slant is unabashadly towards Language Poets and work by poets featured in Eshleman's SULFUR magazine. BERNSTEIN, MICHAEL PALMER, and JED RASULA are contributing editors for SULFUR. RAE ARMANTROUT, SUSAN HOWE, BOB PERELMAN, STEPHEN RODEFER, and JOHN TAGGART all have connections either with the Bay Area language folk or with Burning Deck Enterprises (Providence, R.I.) which specializes in these poets. All but one writer has appeared in SULFUR. *Temblor,* surely a labor of love for the editor, is one of the most narrowly focused of current magazines.

In CLAYTON ESHLEMAN's poems Ariadne, Dionysus, ancient cave painters, Minotaurs, Venus, the Wawilak sisters, Eshleman's own father and mother, Theseus, and Leviathan and Behemoth blend in an amazing mix. Eshleman is one of our few poets with a private mythology: here, for example, a hero blends sperm with "the serpentine / bodies of the Sisters" and "engages them at the haft / of the double labrys . . . ." In "Ariadne's Reunion," Eshleman engages his double, his "other," in lean, straightforward, supple writing, not without irony. After the rejection, the hero is transformed into a woman, his anima, a reflection of Ariadne who is about to appear with "her bull-headed partner." Here are the opening lines:

I was called out into the forest to box
with a man I had been told represented
my other. I wore big blue gloves
and a nose mask. We squared off in a clearing

and remained in that position forever,
for as soon as we recognized the extent to which
we mirrored one another, we both slipped
out our backs,
he to quest with lantern for a younger man,
not that burlesque of virility I had put on.

"Deeds Done And Suffered By Light" is one of Eshleman's best vision/dream pieces, an ambitious recording of a descent into an underworld where he meets his parents. In characteristic fashion, Eshleman displays an uncanny knack for making the invisible visible, ie., the landscape of a Blakean underworld. The parents long for him. He remains their baby, who must still be carefully supervised. The mother's chatter is a delight, part worrying, part delicious, part nagging:

My buttons are mouldy
and my hands have no flesh left but I
still manage
to squeak my buttons a little and get
into your dreams.
I'm sorry if I appear both dead and alive
to you,
but you should know by now you can't have
it your way all
time.

Eshleman engages both mind and emotion--something rare in *Temblor.*

35 (count 'em) fat pages are spent on JOHN TAGGART's "The Rothko Chapel Poem." I assume that Taggart aims for a verse style as "abstract" or "bloodless" as Mark Rothko's painting style. Snore. Snore. Taggart reworks lines like this through a deadly maze: "Red deepened by black red made deep by black /prolation of deep red like stairs of lava/deep like stairs of lava to gether us in" etc. One hungers for "The Boy Stood On the Burning Deck." The best of these takes revolve like slow pin-wheels around a central motif of "scream," certainly an appropriate image for our

obscene times. Here, the effect is like the box within the box, the little Quaker Oats man holding the Quaker Oats man, etc:

Only one scream really it is
only one scream within echoes
itself within the one scream
the one scream within screams
one passionate scream within
been sustained one scream has
being sustained one scream is
in one black room sustained
only one scream within echoes
itself within the one scream
the one scream within screams
will not decay in one scream
in one black room it will not.

As we sort our way through these self-obsessive locked-in personas, the endless boring doors, and the screams, we reach an oasis moment (which can be read as a devastating criticism of Taggart's writing) which promises a good suck of camel milk and a ripe date or two: "It's time to move time for some passion in this language . . . ." The promise is, alas, a mirage, for by line three we are again pinned wriggling to the wall of Taggart's blandness.

MICHAEL PALMER, employs a series of "It is" lines to extol lost books, burning houses, and a "libel of shores" in a sacerdotal melange. The challenge Palmer seems to set up for himself is to evoke a burning world and see how few breaths he requires to locate it. Again, ROTHKO's painting comes to mind. One title would seem to evoke Palmer's ideal poem: "Word That Would Not Be Written."

In Palmer's "The Opening," five brief breaths constitute the whole. Though "momently" echoes "opening" and there is some pleasant long vowel music in stanza four, the evanescent effects are like delicate Whistlerian posturings. And all this, despite the harrowing image of a starving African, so ommnipresent of late on our TV screens--the swollen belly, the primitive bowl, the crust of bread, the violet skin, the flies gathering on lips and eyes:

The Opening

The opening is read by the tongue
momently for the dead now

as they multiply
far from here--are

(as words this high)--are
amid sand the few fragments

bowl bread violet
curve swollen outward

of flies gathered
at lips and eyes

KARIN LESING, another SULFUR poet, rambles much about a Chinese wall, Mary of Vladimir, St. Francis having his dinner, and dreams. Here is a pretentious rumination on what morning means, including the final unhappy image of settling her forehead "among the shining fires." Her start sounds as if she's been assigned a topic for a poem (in some Berkeley workshop?):

Why mornings are dreadful.Why you dread
all mornings.Like beginnings.Their
multiplicity.Their maze of possibilities, thread
and thrum.Make a fresh start, they shout and
already you run and have lost your way . . . ."

Lessing's prose poems are in a genre which derives from women's consciousness raising in the 'sixties--the poems as journal or day-book. Several things bother me:

the sophomoric thinking, viz., the meditation on the dreariness of mornings. Also, the indulgent, flatulent forms which no amount of bircarb can explode. The commonplace linkages. Lessing is best when her vignettes are tiny stories, or evoke a Borges-like dream quality. One of these is "The Attack" where she depicts anger as "ice cold water." Here, in a twilight world vision, this rhyming moment is delicious: "Raspberries, mirabelles . . .! Raise water, raise it from the well . . ."

Japanese poet (b.1919) MINORU YOSHIOKA incorporates flowers, damselflies, gems, and gentle moments we associate with Oriental delicacy--but he presents much more: a world of violence, snakes, castrated goats, and dead horses. He is a marvellous poet, well-translated by ERIC SELLAND. Here he turns reverence-for-the father inside out, lavishing violence and echoes of magical dragon's teeth:

Be joyful at your father's death
Smash the chin with a hammer
And pull out the canine teeth
Go over the weather beaten fields
And throw them inside a possum's den
Along with a pinecone . . . .

Three poems by MICHEL DEGUY follow, translated by BERNARD BADOR. This sentence should turn the dullest of grammar teachers over is his/her grave: "Now is it not a hunger that poetry could also welcome and gratify--at a price of a deception that it alone knows how to handle gingerly?" A typing-exercise gone askew? Obviously, Bador-Deguy desperately need White and Strunk. In another poem, this delicious grammar-sniffing (as in glue-sniffing) occurs, inducing a high so transcendent and abstract it takes moments to come down before proceeding:

You were beating this dose with your fists, this consecution of the irreal of the past (I would have loved) and of the future perfect (to be he who will have been) which makes an irreal of the present (he who would love you).

Poem 3 begins this way:

Limitrophe poetry demands a leap
Which projects onto a border or a ressaut
In the pleasure Lucretius was talking about . . . .

While reading CHARLES BERNSTEIN won't shiver your soul or excite you much, you may enjoy sharing some of his more lucid moments and his lavish puns:

Early
warning sighs. Buttressing broncho-
dilation, arcadian
microseconds jostling pansynchronic obsidian
vases in the
collation of infrequent mention.

Bernstein adorns his long poem with numerous contemporary allusions, most of them dismal in their force-the immanence of nuclear destruction, social injustice (a nation "half poor/and half garbage"), our hostility and/or stupidity towards clear thinking and "plain words"; and much jazzy hip reposturing of pop music and commonplaces, viz.:

The clothier makes the person (there's
a change in the sweater, a change
in the smock, from now on
they'll be a change in *you*).

Here's a tepid cliché, togetherness: we need to recognize that we're in this together and we must respect our "differences"

. . . we 'are' each other only insofar as each
can recognize and acknowledge the differences
(as in separately bodied)--to con*fuse* this risks
a rule of
power only.

Kitsch LEO BUSCAGLIA!

RAE ARMANTROUT's poems sound much like KARIN LESSING's daybook jottings, journal entries--with this difference. Armantrout deletes more, and sets her scribblings in fairly sophisticated-looking verse forms. Her lines, though, too often sound like pompous mottos, set down with little variety, stultified by an endlessly repetitious verb-subject-object pattern. She loves sounding omniscient, and her observations are occasionally presented in self-serving passive voice. These are random samples: "Emphatic / precision/is revealed as/hostility." "A list may pantomime/focus." There are faintly washed genre scenes: a woman does dishes, couples lounge in "fenced yards," morning glory leaves. Little, alas, goes anywhere.

BOB PERELMAN too flings forth imperatives. He's better than Bernstein because he doesn't turn aside for puns. "Cliff Notes" is a powerful piece spoken by a stunned survivor of a lost culture, formerly ours, now demolished by nuclear war. "Traces" of our destroyed universe remain on the cliffs. There's a swift fly-over from SOCRATES to now. The Romans, Perelman says, taught us to "see the sky / artificial creation of the scarcity of meaning / spread out ovr the proletariat as a visible economic ether. / You can look but it costs." Perelman leaves me chilled:

We can still see traces
of the tracts where they lived
and still understand their language,
which consisted entirely of dirty jokes
about money.
It's easy to clear away the froth of biology
with a few words
to reveal the naked ageless windwashed marble
holding still for recorded history.

MICHAEL DAVIDSON, yet another lover of the declarative motto poem, does at least flesh out the abstractions and the syntactical snorkellings with personal touches. In "The Fall(Tentative)" he evokes the joys of ocean-swimming, reports an exchange with a Mr. Wicket who tries to get the opening lines of a poem right, and conjectures on the doomed nature of contemporary civilization. What saves Davidson from language-flight-boredom are his personal moments:

this is where I live
this is my dog
there are other colors
and they live next door.

This observation I'll remember for a long time:

I don't know
words repeated in an empty car
are still words
and I still hear them.

"Unheard songs are sweeter," etc.

DENNIS PHILLIPS also loves the partially heard song. "A World" oscillates over, around, and through a love affair, allowing the merest hints of narrative to emerge. The elusiveness is disturbing, especially since the energies suppressed seem volcanic ("Don't look for me: If the fire escapes/ even hope would vanish."). The poems (there are 13) move in and out of a disturbed love relationship. The most obviously violent poem is the 6th, in which "he" tries to pry an "invisible / jewish skull" off his desk where it has been bolted. It appears also that *he* has been ill, feverish; or, rather, "I" has been ill--the third and first pronouns are interchangeable, engendering some of the vagueness Phillips likes. While persons may not be clear, genders are. Sterility is also an issue--on his penis (the "lipless tiny mouth") there's blood. He's "empty." The "ladder" of the moment (I gather that *he/I* remains an invalid) tips, but neither "Laurel nor/Hardy balance at the top." Is the poem a "masque", or isn't it? Did someone have coffee? Or did no one have coffee? Did the ladder fall? Who is going to forget all this? who remember? Some readers will fall into one basket, I would guess, some in the other. The basket of those who forget will probably be much fuller than the basket of those who remember.

I have written elsewhere [*The Great American Poetry Bake-Off: Second Series*] about HARRY E. NORTHUP's *Enough the Great Running Chapel,* which is excerpted here. Northup performed cartwheels with language and obfuscated meanings long before most of the so-called Language Poets got busy cracking their phonemes and morphemes. Northup, I'd say, has taken his cue from *Finnegan's Wake* rather than from DERRIDA, DEGUY, and J. HILLIS MILLER. Here he riffs conjunctions and adjectives, and since he himself is a successful movie and television actor, evokes some of the glitz and chaos of that world:

grit praise amoral where's, & what about,
the morality
sublime student, hate, a conjunction that
will never be
an adjective
star
turn
kick sage the sets through & slightly above
where it never
can be seen
west corner seams a missing through &
adjectives bleed when
we are about to come
into one another . . . .

Many of the devices I have been lamenting--the boring fascination with how the thing is said rather than with what is said, the pretentious declaratives and soft passive voice constructions, the jottings from day-books--all appear in a pair of poems by PAUL VANGELISTI closing this issue. Vangelisti, one of our finest lyrical poets, transcends the limitations. His secret, I think, is intelligence and esthetic control; he seems to have thought through his tones and modes, and proceeded with his imagination at white heat, controlled by form. In this amazing passage, he confronts himself after being abandoned by a lover, who leaves him devastated, as he takes the train away from her. Line 4 is loaded with the passion he struggles to suppress--he forces a smile, and sees the lover as a mere eyelash on the horizon. yet, he remains harrowingly vulnerable:

she named me though I can't remember what
she said
she dreamt me and it's been weeks since I slept
she tasted me until I am bitter as my smile
she blistered and slaked me slaked and
blistered me till my whispers peeled
like skin
she has left me an eyelash on my own horizon
I stare out the train window north across
the border away from you
a few road signs the names vacant a hutling
round of green upon green.

The second poem "for Giuliano," is from a new series of poems written as letters by the Emperor Hadrian to an assortment of friends. Note the metrical beauty of this quietly commanding prose-poem. The image of sleep as a dropped magazine is superb, as is the concluding ambivalence:

For a moment I was dozing. The ink I write
with is yours.
At table on a hilltop in a room of birdsong and
insect whirr sand
broken clocks, a man and woman sat facing. They
didn't speak of
painting or poetry or even themselves, in fact
it was immpossible
to tell what they were speaking of. The drowsy
current
suspending their talk seemed limitless, somehow
final. My
comments on your drawings will wait. Sleep has
hold and is
about to drop me like a magazine to the table.
In the moment it

takes to turn a page, I may still be within the
flowing room,
perhaps even allowed to overhear.

TEMBLOR. If you want to appear here write about myths, the more obsure the better, do a fair amount of automatic writing, be metaphysical, mention either CHARLES OLSON, ROBERT DUNCAN, or MICHEL DEGUY. If you contribute prose, avoid logic, deftness of tone and style, ie., strive to dislocate your reader and obfuscate him as much as possible. Having appeared first in SULFUR or in WRITING/TALKS or in SAGETRIEB or in the Burning Deck series will also help. If you wish to deviate from the norm, however gently, read PAUL VANGELISTI, HARRY NORTHUP, BOB PERELMAN and DENNIS PHILLIPS for inspiration. Interestingly, all of the good poets but one live in Southern California, evidence of much vigor there, and the possible transfer of the West Coast poetry torch from San Francisco to Los Angeles.

Despite my carpings, I applaud editor Lee Hickman's focus: great journals have pioneered new territory this way, ie., by knowing quite specifically what they were up to. Alas, my feeling is, though, that Hickman spends too much effort, not on charting new ground, but on giving a narrow coterie of poets yet another journal for themselves. Perhaps *Temblor* will still be the earthquake the title suggests it is; my guess is that it is too locked in, "nay," as old THOMAS CARLYLE would have said, even academic. In its way it represents a gaggle of poets everybit as exclusive and repressive as those appearing in APR, FIELD, ANTAEUS, and THE IOWA REVIEW. We need journals that display the considerable variety of American verse today, ones that will include the best of these poets, of the Iowa types, of the WORMWOOD REVIEW poets, and the great independents (there are many around, writing quite oblivious to coteries and schools.)

VISIONS

#14 (1985). Poetry Editor: Bradley R. Strahan, Black Buzzard Press, 4705 S. 8th Road, Arlington, VA 22204. $8.50 per year.

Visions, in its fifth year, is an unpretentious mix of good poetry and good graphics. The editor announces that he wishes to provide a forum for poets "at the heart of the poetic tradition which is out of fashion with most of today's literary gate-keepers." He seeks "lyricism," "sensibility" (not sentimentality), "accessibility" (surface clarity). He complains of the "trendy" in poetry, and looks forward to the time when the pendulum will swing back to poems that people understand. He names no names, alas.

A modest enough goal, and one which editor Strahan fulfills. The poems he admires yield up surface meanings readily, and remind one of a host of magazines around, including *Poetry Now, Bogg, Iowa Review,* and *Hanging Loose.*

The poems are heavily first-person, and several are trivial: JOSEPH HARRIS' bit on hanging his UTRILLO painting; JUDITH GRAD's luxuriating in the tast of soft ice cream. There are also *You Poems,* popularized by Iowa Poets, who tell "you" what "you" thinks, does, etc. These should be strung up by their necks like dead cats, skinned, and sent to Iowa City.

The high points: DOUGLAS SCRIBNER's first views of a girl's breasts. GARY FINCKE's recollection of a boyhood friend. KATHLEEN IDDINGS' bizarre and original "Suckering Tobacco"--sex in the woods with Hank who pulls "fat worms from their hiding places" while Ki pulls suckers from the tobacco. HAROLD BLACK's powerful poem on Moloch. There are good things here. What *Visions* demonstrates is that you can fill a magazine with conservative, unpretentious art and make it work. It's all more than fit "for nature's daily food," as Wordsworth said, if not for the ages.

THE NOISOME BUNNY AWARDS

[0 Bunny]

BEST: THE NEW YORK QUARTERLY, POETRY AUSTRALIA, THE REAPER

[1 Bunny]

GOOD: FRANK, HOME PLANET NEWS, THE MID-AMERICAN REVIEW, PLANET DETROIT, VISIONS

[2 Bunnies]

MIDDLING: CHIAROSCURO, CRAZYHORSE, HANGING LOOSE, ORIGIN, PIKESTAFF FORUM, TEMBLOR

[3 Bunnies]

NOISOME: THE FESSENDEN REVIEW, HARPER'S, OUTLAW, POETRY, POETRY / LA